A Stage Mother's Story

— We're not all Mrs Worthingtons!

by Hazel K. Bell

To Aidan—of course

© *Hazel K. Bell* 2006

ISBN 0-9552503-1-5
ISBN 978-0-9552503-1-6

Printed by Hawke Print Ltd
Welwyn Garden City
Hertfordshire AL7 1BH

HKB Press
139 The Ryde, Hatfield, Herts AL9 5DP

http://www.aidanbell./com/hkbpress/welcome.htm

Contents

		Page
	Preface	5
1	Beside the Seaside	6
2	Aidan Makes His Entrance	8
3	Bringing up Barnstormer	10
4	In Love with a Wonderful Show	16
5	Showy College Days	18
6	Odd Jobs	22
7	An Actor in the House	26
8	Touring the Country	32
9	Priming the Piper	35
10	Musical Muster	40
11	Comrades in Arts	43
12	The Professional Stage Mother	46
13	In Another Part of the Theatre	47
14	From Hatfield to Vienna by Voice	49
15	Margaret Rules!	54
16	Back at the Ranch	56
17	Casting, Casting	58
18	Horror in Hungary	62
19	The Spice of Life	66
20	Soul-searching to Music	69
21	Viennese Ventures	70
22	Rocky II	72
23	Continental Crossings	76
24	Rocky III	80
25	Impresario about Town	82
26	Dear Mrs Worthington . . .	87
	Index	89

Illustrations

The Falcheham Players at Felpham Village Hall, 1947	7
Kay Macaulife in *When We Are Married*, 1966	8
Wannabe child model, 1972	11
Star of The X Theatre: *Billy*, 1975	14
Aidan with chorus ladies from dancing school, 1976	15
Puck in Hatfield School production, *A Midsummer Night's Dream*, 1977	16
Demonstrating steam irons, 1983	23
A morse code user: TV advertisement, 1984	27
Dunking a grapefruit in a tea-cup to make fruit tea: TV advertisement, 1985	28
Simple Simon in *Dick Whittington;* Hampstead, 1984-85	29
A keyboard player in *The Two Ronnies*, 1985	30
Mike the Milkman in *Mother Goose*; Bristol Old Vic, 1985-86	30
A Funny Thing Happened on the Way to the Forum, 1988	31
Aidan as Aunt Spiker with his real-life sister, 1988	32
The Ideal Gnome Expedition, 1989	34
Acornsoft BBC Elite box	36
Piper, Welwyn Garden City, 1987	38
Singing 'Old Fashioned Melody' in *Hair*, 1990	50
Leon Snevets and Margaret Assarowa – aka Noel Stevens and Aidan, 1991	55
Diana as a crew member for the *Rocky Horror Show*; Budapest, 1991	64
Aidan's logo	73
Riff Raff the butler, 1992	74
Riff Raff the extraterrestrial, 1992	75
A couple of song and dance men in *Who The Hell Is Aidan Bell?* 1993	79
Three Riff Raffs: Alexander Goebel, Aidan and Richard O'Brien, 1993	81
Aidan's party trick at the X-ART studio launch, 1993	83
Timewarp CD, 1994	85
The underwater Time Warp, 1994	86
Aidan and his proud mother after *Who the Hell Is Aidan Bell?* 1993	88

Preface

Don't put your daughter on the stage, Mrs Worthington,
Don't put your daughter on the stage

—*Noël Coward*

My middle child's thirtieth birthday was celebrated in a leisure complex in Vienna, attended by some two hundred and fifty guests. During the evening leading up to the midnight toast his first solo CD was launched, with Aidan singing numbers from it on a stage in the centre of the swimming pool, alone save for the band behind him, two television cameramen recording his every move, and two backing singers, one of them his sister. It all seemed an unlikely answer to the question, 'What do you get if you cross a research chemist with an English teacher?'

I did not defy Mr Noël Coward's advice so blatantly as my epigraph suggests. My elder son sat before computers, while my daughter worked front of house in the theatre world, the hither side of the footlights. Nor did I positively *put* my younger son on the stage: rather he seemed perforce to assume his destined place there. But his choice of career made much impact on my own more conventional life as a teacher, then indexer and editor working from home, in Hatfield, Hertfordshire. I think it time that the maternal perspective of life upon the wicked stage should be detailed, if only *pour encourager les autres*.

As the mother of an actor/singer/producer/entrepreneur, would I endorse Mr Coward's cautious, contra-indicatory advice? Read on . . .

1 Beside the Seaside

My family has enthusiastically indulged in amateur drama for at least two generations back. Then my mother, Kay Macaulife, went further, spending some professional years in repertory at the Roof Garden Theatre at the landward end of Bognor Regis pier. I grew up with the theatre, both performance and administration, as a normal part of life.

My parents moved with my small brother and me to the village of Felpham, on the Sussex coast, at the outset of the second world war, and stayed there for thirteen years. Felpham lies two miles east of Bognor, which was then well provided with theatres. The pier boasted two: the Pier Theatre, splendidly traditional with orchestra pit, red velvet curtains and all, offering variety shows; above it, on the upper layer of the pier, the Roof Garden Theatre, with repertory drama companies. Along the promenade to the west, the Esplanade Theatre offered more serious music concerts, as well as reviews played through the summer: *Dazzle* with Eric and Ida Ross, and brother Johnny Ross, holding it for several years. Susan Hampshire hails from Bognor; Julie Andrews as a child often sang at the Esplanade. Doreen ('Pip') Hinton, later featured on the children's television programme, *Blue Peter*, performed regularly at the Pier theatre.

Rosemary Harris is the most distinguished graduate of Bognor Regis repertory theatre. Her first job was there, as assistant stage manager, to pay her way through drama school. Others who went on to make their names were Michael Hawkins and Roland Curram, both much seen subsequently on platform and screen.

My mother, a playwright who produced many one-act plays with all-women casts, very popular with Townswomen's Guilds and Women's Institutes, joined the Roof Garden Theatre repertory company – the Phoenix, then the Buskin Players. She was Company Secretary, and also played on stage in alternate weeks (depending on casting requirements, of course). Each week the company was performing one play in the evenings, rehearsing another in the mornings.

I had a stage-struck childhood, seeing the Rosses' revues most Saturdays in summer, and hanging round the repertory theatre, making tea for rehearsals and selling programmes for performances, adoring the actors. I even made it on to the Roof Garden stage when a child was needed, once as Tiny Tim, and occasionally as a dancer; then, later, standing in for the youngest member of the company when she was ill. My school holidays at age 15 were spent as assistant to the A.S.M. at the Rep theatre, happily 'propping' – searching for and begging to borrow props needed for performances. My diary for that year ends, "I MUST go on the stage!"

Both my parents also played in the revues put on by The Falcheham Players in Felpham Village Hall, with me sometimes in the child parts. One of these was the dreadful schoolgirl, Monica, played by Beryl Reid in the radio comedy, *Educating Archie;* another, Sophie Tuckshop from *ITMA*, declaring after the interval, 'I thpat in all the coffeeth'.

I attended dancing classes offering tap and 'modern': the Joan Leonard School, then Joan Newnham's, then some years with Daphne Willmer, formerly one of the Clarkson Rose dancing troupe. Classes were held in a room over a Felpham pub, 'The George'. Once a fortnight in the summer a coach took us all to the Elmer Sands Holiday Camp, five miles east, where we sang and danced for the holidaymakers—unsophisticated entertainment indeed by today's standards. I recall my artless solos, 'It's Foolish But It's Fun', 'When the Sun Shines Everyone Makes Hay', 'Happy Feet'. We also danced at local concerts and fêtes, and put on pantomimes. I entered frequent talent competitions, tap dancing, singing or reciting – the latter surely a lost performance art now? On many a stage I declaimed James Whitcomb Riley's 'Little Orphan Annie came to our house to stay' (each verse ending, 'And the gobble-ums will get you if you don't watch out!'), or 'The Fly in Church' by Jocelyn Lea, with its pathetic conclusion, 'Oh friend for little children, you were once a child like me ... Be sorry for a little boy and send another fly'. It came to be my proud boast that I had performed on every stage in and around Bognor Regis.

Once, eager to read the local papers' reviews of a pantomime I had played in, I was puzzled to read that I had given 'a suave performance'. A word unencountered before: what could it mean? Still waiting for the other local paper to be delivered to the bookstall, I could not rush home to ask my mother. Finally unable to wait longer to learn what was being written of me, I turned to the strange man behind me in the queue to ask, 'Please, what does syoo-aive mean? – because I'm it'.

Now, alas, the Elmer Sands Club is no more, and a huge Butlin's Holiday Camp sprawls between Bognor and Felpham. The Roof Garden Theatre has become a

The Falcheham Players at Felpham Village Hall, 1947; Kay Macaulife centre stage

Kay Macaulife as Clara Soppitt in Priestley's *When We Are Married* with the Wimbledon Repertory Theatre Players, 1966

billiards hall; the Pier Theatre area houses yet another amusement arcade—already Bognor had several, stretching along the promenade from Pier to Arcade, and they remain still. The Esplanade Theatre is just not there. Bognor's only theatre now is part of the Regis Centre Complex; sad contrast to such wonderful theatre supply in the forties and fifties.

No such seaside, pier shows, revues and village fêtes for my own three children, brought up far inland in Hertfordshire New Town district in the sixties and seventies. Having grown up myself taking for granted the beach at the bottom of the garden in Felpham, village community life, and visits to theatres every week, I felt my children much deprived.

2 Aidan Makes His Entrance

Leaving university already married, I abandoned thoughts of a stage career, and settled where my husband, Colin, had taken work as a research chemist, in Welwyn Garden City, Hertfordshire, in London's commuter belt. I took to teaching, until we should start a family. I decided to return to the amateur stage, and joined the local musical dramatic society. In the week of the auditions for *Oklahoma*, though, with my sights fixed on the role of Ado Annie, I found I was pregnant, and abandoned teaching and am dram alike in favour of child rearing. There's portentous for you.

Our first child, Ian, was born conventionally enough, in hospital, on All Saints Day, 1962 (in the aftermath of the near-US-invasion of Cuba, the Bay of Pigs. I expected to give birth in an air-raid shelter). Aidan, however, made his entrance into the world on May Day, 1964, with what was to become typical public notice and confusion.

We had moved three miles from Welwyn Garden City to live in Hatfield, on a new estate that lacked road-name signs, road surfaces, pavements, and neighbours: a pioneering existence. No house numbers yet allotted, either: we resorted to calling our bungalow 'Carillon'.

Shortly before our second baby was due, another woman moved in nearby, and I called to invite her in for coffee. She was not free then, but mentioned, looking at my obvious signs of late pregnancy, that she had once been a nurse and would be happy to help with the baby if ever she was needed.

At that time, second births, when the first had not been medically complicated, had to be at home. My mother came to stay when the birth was due, to look after toddler Ian. I went into labour in the early evening, and called the midwife, who arrived and told me crossly that it was much too early for her attentions to be needed: I should take two aspirins and go to bed, and she would come again in the morning.

When I staggered to the bathroom at ten o'clock next morning it was very apparent that the midwife was urgently needed—but at that time midwives travelled by bicycle, and had no radio contact. Mine was by then out on her rounds and we could not reach her. Colin carried me back to bed (with an arm in plaster after falling from the loft while installing the wiring for our new bungalow), and I told him, 'The woman with a yellow front door used to be a nurse—get her'. Colin went off to knock on the yellow door, introduced himself and explained; with superb calm our new neighbour—Dorothy, as it turned out—said, 'I've just been washing up—my hands are quite clean', crossed the road and delivered Aidan. My mother, looking after Ian in the garden, unaware of the sudden crisis, saw Dorothy's arrival and thought, 'How kind—a neighbourly enquiry. Perhaps I should offer her a cup of tea'. She came into the bedroom asking politely, 'Can I do anything for you?', and was urgently told 'Yes—hold this leg'.

Colin rang our doctor, who came out of his surgery, looked round the waiting room, said 'None of you are urgent—I'm going to a new baby'. He left the would-be patients and came straight to us. After examining Aidan, he rang the county Midwives Department to complain, insisting that the Midwifery Supervisor come to join us. When our designated midwife eventually arrived she found a crowded room: the doctor, her own Supervisor, Dorothy, my mother with Ian, Colin, the baby and me all awaiting her arrival. 'Oh', she said, 'I thought I'd do my urgent calls first'.

The crowd dispersed, and the midwife filled out the birth record (B.B.A.—Born Before Arrival), having to ask us what was the baby's sex.

Aidan had made a dramatic start, and drawn his first crowd.

3 Bringing up Barnstormer

The first signs were early, that the family tradition of stage-striding was coming to a head with Aidan. It was a noisy childhood. Favourite toys were xylophone and drums; also glove puppets, constantly animated. For his puppet booth we converted half of a hexagonal play-pen, for which I made a colourful cover from curtains, sewing stars and animal shapes onto it. He loved dressing, making-up and acting as a clown, at home and away.

Aidan's first appearance on a public stage was as the Sword Bearer with the local amateur operatic society, in *The Mikado*. He wordlessly followed the Executioner round the stage, and loved it all. He then progressed to singing and dancing in *The Wizard of Oz* at the Barn Theatre Club. His early hero was not John Wayne or James Bond, but Fred Astaire. I greatly enjoyed taking him to see Astaire films whenever shown locally.

Attempts to secure child modelling work led to the knowledge that women attending their young are dismissed categorically (and contemptuously) as 'the mother' in the stage and modelling worlds— just as in maternity wards. Aidan loved his session of photographs in a variety of costumes, aged six, telling the photographer eagerly, 'I want to be famous'; a declaration from which he has never wavered.

I took Aidan often to the Little Angel Marionette Theatre in Islington, a mile north-east of King's Cross. When they ran a competition for child puppeteers, he devised a scenario based on the children's book, *Little Blue and Little Yellow*, using lights that shone through cellophane circles on sticks. I recorded the Valse from Walton's *Façade Suite* on tape to accompany this, as being suitably delicate, playful music. Burdened with props and cassette-player, we wheeled the playpen-booth along Islington High Street.

The show we watched before the competition, unfortunately, was accompanied by the same music from *Façade*, and I wanted to stand up and yell, 'It's not plagiarism! We thought of it ourselves!'. Anyway, Aidan won the competition.

We spent some months from 1972-73 in Princeton, New Jersey. While we were there, Aidan performed puppet shows for the children in the University Faculty apartment block we were staying in, and took drum lessons from a student. He and Ian attended Riverside Junior School. Aidan's class performed a moral play about a lazy boy who decides not to get up in , wherehe morning, then meets representatives from every layer of creation, from lowly insects up to the sun, to learn that they all must get up each day and do their work. Aidan, in my orange bathrobe and a cardboard head-dress, was the sun. An American father behind us muttered, 'Wouldn't you know it—even the sun has a British accent!'

Like Mike in *A Chorus Line* ('I Can Do That'), Aidan attended his sister's dancing class, as the only boy. These demographics led to many a concert appearance for him flanked by dancing girls.

My children's dancing classes were very different from my own: not held over a pub, but in a Welwyn Garden City hall; not performing at holiday camps and

Wannabe child model, 1972

pantomimes, but giving serious, lengthy displays of national dancing at Welwyn Garden City's Campus West Theatre. The girls wore black skirts and leotards: an amazing number of national variations could be achieved by additions to this basic costume. To forestall the temptation of the parental audience to leave quietly after their own daughter had appeared, each child performed both before and after the interval.

Through these years I costumed many a role from my own wardrobe. I unpicked the pocket-badge from my old university blazer and cut it down to make an Astaire-type mini-tail-jacket (in which Aidan won a fancy-dress competition, dancing with a cane in the parade). I particularly regretted the sacrifice of a pair of black tights to sew a white cut-out skeleton down them for a dance in *The Wizard of Oz*. Many were the miles driven, to drama classes (in St Albans, seven miles away, after school), clubs, rehearsals and productions . The choice was then whether to hang around waiting for the event to be over to drive Aidan home again, or to let it take four trips altogether – there, home again, return to collect Aidan, and home again, home again, joggety-jog ...

Aidan showed an early sense of proper respect for professionalism as distinct from amateur enthusiasm, at a children's show at the Young Vic. When the entertainer asked for young singers from the audience to come on to the stage, and I urged my son, 'Why don't you go up?' he grumbled, 'I came here to see a show. I don't call me going up on stage and singing, seeing a show'.

He developed early a fascination with recording, and nearly caused the abrupt closure of a performance at the Barn Theatre he was helping with backstage, when the stage manager noticed a puzzling black box with trailing wires, and suspected a planted bomb. Aidan heard the anxious whispered consultations of the stage crew, and owned up – he was attempting to record the performance for himself.

Aidan joined the church choir, and Saturdays became taken up by driving him to weddings to sing and earn a few pence—less than the cost of the petrol to get him there and later collect him. This set the pattern for financial dealings involving Aidan for many years to come.

The church choir led to my closest experience of the feudal system. Our local great house invited – or summonsed— the choirboys to sing carols round their tree each Christmas Eve: parental escort was permitted. Thinking this my one chance to witness the private festivities of the mighty, I rescheduled our Christmas Eve meals, apologized to our guests, and set off with Aidan through the snow to the heavy park gates, where our small band gathered, stamping and shivering. At last the custodian admitted us and we trudged on to the house itself, where the grand family and their guests were assembled round a large fir tree in the vast Tudor hall.

We humble parents of the choir, still in our coats, shuffled to a bench at the far end, like a group from a Thomas Hardy novel.

Smoke billowed into the room from a blazing hearth. Scions of the aristocracy drifted round the Christmas tree, lighting real candles in its branches. The Spirit of Monty Python's Upper Class Twit contest rather than of Charles Dickens seemed to hover over us as one young gentleman inadvertently set one young lady's hair afire, and it was patted out with shrill cries. Our lads sang, and were rewarded with presents taken from the tree (their labels read out with some difficulty by the lordlings), orange juice and a mince pie apiece.

The peasant parents sat in their row, gazing on it all, longing for mince-pies and hot drinks; but such thoughts were presumptuous. We received no more than a gracious hand-shake from an unnamed lady. Our vicarious contribution to the feast was over, and off we shuffled into the night. God keep us all in our estate.

Later, one mother of a choirboy found that one of the aristocratic pet dogs had fouled her son's cassock. It took many laborious washings on her part to get rid of the noble canine smell.

Aidan periodically invited local children to attend his own shows in his bedroom: crowded, however small the audience. At the age of ten he commandeered our garage, hanging curtains there, selling cloakroom tickets for pennies through the backless tool cupboard in the garage wall, and assembling the children in rows to watch shows in 'The X Theatre' (described in a handbill as 'a small but life-size theatre'). There was always an eager assistant — schoolfriend or neighbour. In the interval, the audience were offered orange-squash ice cubes frozen in trays in our fridge – one cube each. After the shows favoured children were allowed to queue outside Aidan's bedroom window, stage-door style, to be handed signed scraps of paper by Aidan resplendent in gold-lapelled purple dressing-gown.

The X Theatre's opening production was *Billy*; not likely to be confused with the Michael Crawford production that inspired it. The X Theatre version was performed by Aidan alone, 'with Robert Brook as lighting associate and sound technician'. The programme boasted, '1 Whole hour of Immense Enjoyment ... Please come,————-youl love it!!!!!!!!', but warned, 'children over 10 will not like it', and, 'All children under 4 must be accompanied by a responsible person. Aidan has the right to turn out any hooligans and missbehaving persons!!!!'

Subsequent X Theatre productions included *Bunny and the Birthday Tree, Pinocchio's Christmas, The Play Away Play, The Mystery of the Vanishing Teapot, Bam Bo Be Bom Bay,* and *Welcome 78* ('a traditional Christmas pantomime, featuring a panto dame, oh no it wasnt, oh yes it was, and a cooking scene', with cast of two). *Encore X Theatre* was billed as 'the X Theatres 10.th Production. (Excluding the lecture given by Aidan last month)'. The most regular member of the audience was presented with an award, a glass painted gold: this 'gold cup' proudy remained on her parents' mantelpiece for some months.

There are many Roman remains in St Albans (formerly Verulamium), including a one-time Roman theatre, still so named. I took Aidan to see this. He looked around with contemptuous disappointment at the sloping green field, and asked, 'Where's the lighting box?'

His love of music and performance increased, and we felt we must provide him with a piano at home. These instruments are hugely expensive to purchase new, difficult to come by second- (or subsequent-) hand. However, we found ourselves part of a local syndicate passing pianos down a chain. At the top end, keen local musician friends were buying a new one, and were willing to pass on their old one free to friends in return for assistance with the removal process. We were not these next in the chain; four households were involved, each passing down their old piano to receive a superior

13

Star of
The X Theatre:
Billy, 1975

one; we were the bottom end, receiving the oldest piano in return for Colin's labours. The team of five fathers heaving the four pianos around the district must have been the most highly qualified to have undertaken such labour: graduates all, four PhDs. One piano had to be manipulated to the third floor of the building (and its predecessor, down). At the end of the day, they all felt they had truly suffered for art.

Aidan began to develop an interest in writing music. He proudly played us his first composition. Colin pointed out a certain resemblance to a theme from Beethoven's choral symphony. Indignantly Aidan assured us that he had never heard that work, and 'It just shows that Beethoven and I thought the same way'.

By the time for choice of secondary school, Aidan's future career was clear, and we wondered about a stage school. Visiting one that he could have travelled to daily from home, we were shown with so much pride, framed on the wall, the O-level certificates once attained by a glorified pupil, that we reverted to state education, and Aidan attended a local comprehensive. He most enjoyed there the music and drama, participating in many school plays and playing percussion in orchestras. His performances included the parts of Puck in the school play, one of Noah's sons in *Noyes Fludde* in the local church, and 'The Little Drummer Boy' in St Albans cathedral. He also played percussion in the Hertford Symphony Orchestra. The assistant at the men's outfitters from whom we sought to buy him the prescribed wear for all the male players had been incredulous: 'You want to buy a *black suit* for *a boy of fourteen*?' Aidan continued to play with the HSO until 1981, playing in all in more than twenty-one concerts.

Aidan's twelfth birthday, a Saturday, coincided with the first full-day, far-away meeting I had to attend as an editor. I presented him with an LP of Louis Armstrong and a drum kit, gave him a birthday kiss, and departed, leaving Colin to enjoy Aidan's loud birthday celebrations.

Once we realized we were rearing an actor, I recalled my own early theatre ambitions, and what preparations I had thought necessary to fulfil them. I had taught myself three skills I might have to practise on stage: whistling, smoking, and snapping my fingers. I did not feel maternally bound to impart these to Aidan, but did concentrate on diction for all three children, in the face of the dreadful 'er'ferdsher mumble all around us. Driving round Herts, I would make them enunciate distinctly, with seven different vowel sounds, an aspirate and a sibilant, 'Where are we? We're in Ware—yess'; rather than the likely local variant, 'Ware are we? Ware in Ware—yeah'.

Birthday treats were always, inevitably, visits to West End musicals. I only occasionally got to choose which; an early selection was so successful that Aidan insisted on *Billy* for three consecutive years. On his 14th birthday I made it *A Chorus Line*, having heard how marvellous the dancing was, and loth to sit through *Billy* yet again. We took the young girl next door with us. As the show's blue language reverberated round us, I kept thinking defensively, 'The dancing's so good, I'd have brought Aidan even if I'd known – but Sally . . . ?' After learning how she sang 'Tits and Ass' to her parents over breakfast the next day, I could hardly bear to look over the garden fence to meet her mother's eye.

We could never simply leave the theatre when the show was over, and go home, like the crowds. Always Aidan had to wait to watch the musicians finish playing, then rush to the stage door to see whom he could meet. After one visit to *Evita*, Gary Bond

Aidan with chorus ladies from dancing school, Welwyn Garden City, 1976

15

Puck in Hatfield School production, *A Midsummer Night's Dream*, **1977**

was a particular quarry. The stage door keeper told us there was no chance of Aidan's seeing him as he was in conference with Tim Rice. A lucky opening for Aidan: his Head Master had once taught at a school that Rice attended. Aidan assured the keeper that he had a message for Tim Rice 'from his Head Master' (who had once said airily that Aidan might pass on his good wishes should he ever meet Rice). With proper respect for educational authority, the keeper allowed Aidan through, and spent the next forty minutes telling me all the details of his family, while Rice and Bond were eagerly cornered by Aidan.

4 In Love with a Wonderful Show

Aidan then developed a huge enthusiasm for *Jesus Christ Superstar*, showing us another aspect of theatre life: the obsessed fan. I was the first of us to see this show, and did not then much enjoy it. I never buy London theatre programmes, thinking the price iniquitous as well as inequitable, and registering my disapproval as well as practising economy by non-purchase. On this occasion, though, the lack of a programme meant I was baffled throughout. The sheer volume of the sound in the Palace Theatre production made the subtlety and wit of Tim Rice's lyrics, that I so appreciate since, imperceptible. I could not identify characters, and was particularly baffled by Herod—who was this outrageous creature posturing on an airbed? Not in my Bible ... However, I thought that Aidan, who was greatly interested in stage technology, would find the lighting effects, many projected up through a transparent

16

floor, fascinating. I offered to take him: Aidan was loth to attend what he thought would prove to be a Sunday-school morality play, but once in the audience he was totally captivated by the rock music and performance. Eventually, through his teenage years, he went to see this show on its London run more than twenty times. Always he stayed by the stage door afterwards to meet the cast, and collected souvenirs of all sorts: programmes; every record version produced; autographs; photographs. A local paper featured his obsession under the heading, 'Superstar's Superfan'.

Aidan even met his future wife, Conny Heim, at the *Superstar* stage door. She was an equally ardent fan of musicals, coming over to London from her native Germany each summer to see all the London shows she could.

Aidan and Conny also met at that stage door a fat American boy, whom they thought distinctly odd, who said he was in England for the summer working in a London toy shop. At his insistence Conny took photos of him, one together with Barrie James, who played Herod. He asked Barrie James, with extraordinary naivety, whether the masses of jewellery he wore in the role were real. Later, when John Lennon was shot, and Mark Chapman's picture was in all the papers as the killer, Aidan recognized him as the boy he had met at the stage door; the photographs indeed appeared identical. I took ours to our local police station, as evidence of Chapman's presence then in London and tendency to hang round musical performers. I was told to send the photos to the New York Police. I did, and received a strange letter from Captain James C. Power averring that 'ocular and other evidence' showed that the boy in our pictures was not Chapman, and that he was known then to be elsewhere. Since then, though, Fenton Bresler's book, *The murder of John Lennon* (Sidgwick and Jackson), has shown that Chapman was indeed in London that summer (1980), and visited that show and its cast members.

When *Superstar* finished its eight-year run at the Palace Theatre, in August 1980, Aidan managed to attend both the final performance and the party afterwards. Next day, Sunday, at the get-out, he secured more than a hundred of the front-of-house photographs and posters, the conductor's baton, some music sheets and props. He phoned home and persuaded his father to drive to London and load his car with these memorabilia, which subsequently filled Aidan's bedroom and our garage. Herod's airbed finally came to rest spread over the floor of our garden shed.

Superstar was to be followed at the Palace Theatre by *Oklahoma*. The cross which rises from beneath the stage for *Superstar* was found difficult to dismantle. 'Never mind', suggested David Land, the producer; 'Tim [Rice] can write a crucifixion into *Oklahoma*'.

Superstar went on tour, and Aidan into action. He obtained a copy of the tour schedule, and travelled to see the last night at every town it played. I acquired a collection of British Rail timetables, and became an adept journey-planner. The role of Judas was sung by Colm Wilkinson, who lived in London, and was particularly kind about giving Aidan lifts homewards. We met him in the small hours at a variety of venues for the hand-over of our son.

Aidan applied to the theatres where *Superstar* was to play for jobs during the school holidays, succeeding in getting work as a steward for *Superstar*'s run at the Bristol Hippodrome—his first period of living away from home. With a developing

17

sense of self-promotion, he managed to be interviewed on Radio 2 when it covered the Manchester opening of the tour, as the show's most ardent fan. He agreed enthusiastically to the interviewer's question, did he want a career in musicals himself? Yes, he said, as a singer. We still failed to realize all that lay ahead.

5 Showy College Days

In lieu of staying at school for the sixth form, Aidan elected for two years' drama course at a College of Further Education. We did the rounds, and were particularly impressed by one Head of Department, discussing a suitable combination of courses for Aidan. 'If he's going to be an actor, he'll need O-level maths', he told us. 'He'll be working on supermarket check-outs in all the periods of unemployment.'

It came down to a choice between two colleges: North Herts, in Hitchin, an easy rail journey from home, where Aidan could have studied for A-level music; and East Herts, near Broxbourne, fourteen miles away with no direct public transport link, and no music department. The drama department at East Herts, though, was then reckoned superior to all others in the county. Aidan opted for that one, and we faced two more years of parental chauffeuring. Soon after he started there, in 1980, Aidan's interest in music, particularly composition, escalated, and he ignored his examination subjects (English, Theatre Studies and Social Studies) to compose musicals. He provided the music for all the college productions, composing original numbers and accompanying them on piano or keyboards. He almost compensated for the college's lack of music courses, as a one-student music department, and continued to write for them and return to provide musical accompaniment for their productions for some years after he had left the college.

The drama course consisted in great part of putting on shows in all sorts of environments, including touring school halls and open-air fetes. Much use was made of modern audience-integration by having the actors enter from the rear of the auditorium, making frequent forays back into it. Seated in the audience, craning my neck to look behind and around me, I often felt like echoing Aidan's cross childhood comment on being invited onto the stage: 'I came here to see a show. I don't call having the cast rush about in the rows behind me, seeing a show'.

The college was an early practitioner of integrated casting. An outstandingly talented student in the year following Aidan's was a black girl from north London. She gave a splendid performance in *Cabaret* as Sally Bowles, but her talk of her Surrey background, class-conscious mother and Cheltenham education seemed to me incongruous.

I saw Aidan crucified in the college production of *Godspell*, and can report this to be a most harrowing experience for a mother (and indeed for a young sister – Aidan's had nightmares about it for years afterwards), however aware of costumes and scenery and friendly with all concerned. While we shuddered, though, Aidan was dismayed to find how little moved some of the audience were by his supposedly crucified corpse being borne through the auditorium by the other males of the cast, shoulder-high, loin-cloth draped. 'Isn't he thin!' was one penetrating whisper; another, 'I've seen more meat in a corned-beef sandwich'.

One lunch hour in his first year at the college, 1980, a girl student packed five fellow students, Aidan among them, into her new car, intending (illicitly) to take them to her home to see her new puppy – and drove them all into a ditch. Both car doors jammed, and black smoke poured from the bonnet. The boys had to clamber out one by one through a window, and embraced in relief when all were gathered safely at the roadside. A week later, another student passed the spot and was told by his driver, 'There was an accident here last week—it was a carful of queers': very much a categorization of its time.

The first musical Aidan composed, *Piper*, was written in partnership with a fellow student at East Herts college, Brian Phillips, as lyricist. It was based on the legend of the Pied Piper of Hamelin, a story perhaps leading to expectations of a children's musical, but its score is in fact complex, sophisticated, and difficult to perform. This discrepancy may account for the troubles this show has always encountered in getting produced.

The college loved it, and gave *Piper* its first performance as its annual public production, at the Intimate Theatre, Palmers Green, in 1982. The Branchline Theatre Company produced it at Edmonton in the same year; the college, again, two years later.

Aidan was much concerned with presentation and merchandizing. For the college's *Piper* production in 1984, tee-shirts were printed with a logo on the front of the Piper, a flying piper designed by a college student, and on the back, for each member of the production team, the name of the part they played or their function—'Mayor', 'Mayor's Wife', 'Musical Director', 'Composer'. Aidan refused to provide me with one with the slogan, 'Composer's Mother', much though I was involved, particularly in providing transport.

During college vacations Aidan continued to perform his puppet shows. They increased in sophistication, and were offered for pay for children's parties and school entertainments, with an eye to clocking up contracts towards the much-desired Equity card for when he should enter his chosen career. Several contracts were needed for this, without which actors could not be cast in major productions. The contracts had to be gained by working in provincial theatres, on overseas tours, or individual enterprises such as Aidan's. We pushed the playpen-booth along many a path on its little castor wheels. To offer supporting evidence for the contracts I had to take photographs, leaning from upstairs windows to obtain carefully angled pictures that would show at once Aidan, recognizably, behind the booth set up in someone's garden; puppets in performance; and a real, enthralled audience—larger, we hoped the photos would suggest, than the few children the camera sometimes had to record.

A teacher friend asked to have Aidan visit her school in Marlborough to perform to 'three or four classes'. I drove him the sixty miles, car laden with booth and accoutrements, to find that the classes were in fact to attend a separate performance each. After four performances, without his usual devoted young assistant, unable herself to take the day off school to help him, Aidan was exhausted, and told me he

19

had never done such a hard day's work in his life. Then a fifth, unexpected teacher came in, beaming, asking, could she bring her class in now, please . . . ?

One Saturday lunchtime Aidan went up to the loft to get some semi-retired puppets down for that afternoon's party booking. As he was coming down, the ladder slipped and he fell; the loft trap-door closed on his hand, slicing off the top of one finger. Family crisis: son on the hall floor, finger-tip still in loft. I rushed Aidan to the cold tap and bandaging, while Ian went up to the loft to retrieve the piece of finger for possible reattachment. It fell to the ground, whereupon the family cat showed great interest. Ian hastened down the ladder to beat the cat to his brother's finger. Colin and I rushed Aidan to hospital, finger-piece wrapped with ice, leaving sister Diana, typically, to mop up the blood, and Ian to ring the birthday party booker and say that Aidan could not after all come and perform for their young guests. The dismayed hosts suggested that Ian might come and entertain for them instead, but this was not an option.

At casualty we had to wait literally for hours; only one doctor was on weekend duty, and a coronary patient was being treated. We could barely restrain ourselves from banging the desk and crying, 'Our son is a pianist': melodramatic but true. The severed piece 'died' during the waiting, and Aidan now has one finger slightly short.

Ian had failed to explain in full the reason for the puppets' cancellation, and it seemed hard, after returning from our very fraught afternoon at the hospital, and phoning to apologise to the party hosts, to be angrily reproached for 'a bloody disgrace'.

Aidan's career began to move in most effectively on my own equipment for freelance work, especially the answerphone. As a freelance editor and indexer, working from home, I was anxious to have the services I offered detailed on this; also the names of the two journals I edited, to confirm to callers that this private house was indeed their editorial address. When Aidan began earning both money and Equity contracts from his party shows, he pointed out that hostesses who had been told they could get children's entertainment through a certain phone number, and on ringing it heard talk of learned publishing, would assuredly conclude they had the wrong number and seek another puppeteer. I agreed to add children's entertainments to the telephone list of services tendered. Ian was writing his own computer games, and had published two ('Othello' and 'Free Fall'), also based at home, so it was only fair to mention this. And Diana, training to be a Nursery Nurse, was earning money as a much-requested babysitter . . . our phone message came to offer a huge variety of services, a one-family Yellow Pages, and many a caustic reply was found on replaying messages—'What about a military band?'; 'I want a brain operation, can you oblige?'

Aidan's final exams at East Herts College came round, in 1982, contrasting with the academic rigour of the format of his brother's. For the Guildhall School of Music and Drama Diploma (L.G.S.M.D.), he had to play various roles. One required a false moustache: mother was sent to obtain the necessary glue. Chemist after chemist was convulsed by my request, which seemed to lack educational authenticity.

On the day of one exam, I drove Aidan to the college, confident that he was word-perfect and well rehearsed in Romeo's final speech in the Capulet monument. As we sped along the motorway, though, there came the shattering enquiry—'I've just remembered I have to discuss the whole play with the examiner as well as perform the speech, and I haven't read it. What happens in *Romeo and Juliet*?'

A one-time English teacher, I then gave the lesson of my life, at the wheel, without benefit of text to hand, fielding questions such as, 'Wait a minute —which side is Mercutio on? . . . Who did you say Paris was?' When I came to, 'So Romeo dies, and then . . .' I was spared further effort by, 'That's all right—I'll tell the examiner I identified so strongly with Romeo that I didn't want to know what happened after he died'. I am proud to report that Aidan passed that exam *with higher marks for the discussion than for the performance.*

The East Herts class of 1982 left the college to enter the dreadfully competitive world of the theatre, whether, like Aidan, they insisted on launching straight into the search for stage work, or whether they tried for places at Drama Schools—even harder to win, in the face of even greater odds. Brian Phillips got into the Royal Academy of Dramatic Art, duly studied, graduated, and subsequently did very well both as actor and writer, as Brian Jordan.

The class included several highly talented performers, but some fell by the way at this crucial stage. One girl singer failed to win a place, and entered the police force instead. Two excellent dancers won places; one at three different Drama Schools. Both then had to reaudition before their local County Education Authorities to apply for discretionary grants, which both were refused. It seemed extraordinary that local councillors should consider their judgement of dancers keener than that of the Drama School Boards. The denial of grants cost both students their hard-won places; neither could afford to pay their way through Drama School for another two years, and both went straight to the rounds of auditions and what work they could get. Others who failed to get Drama School places this first time round waited to try again the following year.

A boy of great dramatic ability who was not awarded a place at any Drama School refused to contemplate trying again. In a despairing 'see-what-you-made-me-do' gesture, he worked for a year shifting stock in a supermarket. At last he emerged from there, but to the staid recesses of a tax office where he remained for several years, his admirable theatre talent buried beneath a bureaucratic bushel.

The second musical that Aidan wrote with Brian Phillips was *Aesop*, which musically dramatized several of the fables. It was performed at East Herts College after Brian and Aidan had left, in 1983; they returned to produce the show. My research abilities were called into play to find a kazoo—an obscure Australian instrument that Aidan wanted to use for the march of the ants. This mouth-organ-like device was not serious enough to be stocked by shops selling musical instruments, nor frivolous enough for toy shops. After several phone calls and enquiries, and a recommendation to try a museum we could not get to in the time, I gave up, and Aidan resorted to making Dudley-Moore-like noises through a paper and comb. The band was five-piece, but the pianist, Kirk Duncan, broke his wrist some days before the show. The musicians moved round; the now effectively one-handed Kirk played bass on the sample keyboard while Aidan took his place at the piano, two-handed, but needing then to fix the comb to his face to blow through for the ants' march. A condom over the nose proved the most efficient means to hold it in place; but for the school children's matinée the next day it was thought better to replace this with a less efficient rubber band and several frantic grabs.

The organizer of a children's drama festival came to see the matinée, to consider mounting a production of *Aesop*. Aidan asked me to act as hostess to her. She was a very large lady, and when she sailed to the front row and settled herself in the centre, so many dismayed squeals came from the small occupants of the rows behind that I could not bring myself to sit beside her as a second screen, and withdrew to the back.

Ian came to see the performance of *Aesop*, shortly after graduating from Cambridge. East Herts was putting it on for its own end-of-year ceremonies, and after the show the exam results and diplomas achieved by students were announced and presented, with the *Aesop* audience still seated in their rows. The embryonic actors swaggered up to claim their rewards, to the cheers, stamps and whistles of their friends. It was very different from the sombre academic gowns, Latin phrases, bows and handshakes of the Cambridge ceremony, and Ian appeared duly astounded.

For another musical Aidan wrote for the college Diana was lyricist. This was *On Location*, performed there in 1987, about filming commercials in a stately home with genuine English butler. Some years later we were surprised to see the same plot used on television, in Penelope Keith's series, *To The Manor Born*.

6 Odd Jobs

Aidan would devote no further time to education, to delay his assault upon the stage. Work, though, came slowly and oddly. Actors' periods of unemployment and alternative short-term occupations are notorious. Thus, leaving FE college at eighteen, Aidan joined the masses who buy *The Stage* newspaper each week, as early as it can be obtained, and scan the columns frantically looking for auditions open to non-Equity members. Shows find their casts by three types of audition: invitation to individual actors to show themselves, selected by personal reputation or by agents approached as middle-men; Equity-only auditions (the majority); and open ones —always crowded, both within the theatre and down the road outside, with perhaps a 4% chance of selection. Candidates take a large slice out of their non-working day to travel, wait, wait, wait, perform, and travel home, paying their own fares, of course. Aidan was lucky at least in living in the commuter belt, near enough to London to make day trips thither quite reasonable, though expensive on no salary.

He had many photographs of himself taken to mail to agents and producers, with his name printed beneath. 'Aidan' is a fine old Christian name—that of the seventh-century Irish Saint who brought Christianity to Northumbria, indeed. Nevertheless, it is often misspelled by those thinking rather of the Middle Eastern port. One batch of 200 glossy half-plates Aidan had ordered arrived with AIDEN BELL printed large beneath each. The photographers admitted their fault, and supplied another 200 photographs, correctly printed, free. This left us with 200 photographs that could not be sent to agents, and insufficient aunts and cousins to receive them all

22

as gifts. Aidan papered a wall of his room with his own image.

An early job of Aidan's was as a bluecoat at a holiday camp, enabling me to tell friends, 'One of my sons is reading maths at Cambridge; the other is reading Bingo cards at Clacton'. Our family holidays had mostly been spent camping in France (with Aidan putting on puppet shows for the children on the site), but I had to see Aidan entertaining professionally, and his young sister was delighted at the chance of such an unaccustomed holiday. Colin would not contemplate a sojourn in such a place, so I booked a week for myself, daughter and daughter's friend (just returned from a tour with her parents of Greek classical sites, now further extending her cultural horizons). I spent most of the time ensconced in my chalet, working on the journal I was editing. (I had confided my address for the duration to contributors and colleagues with some blushes.)

It was depressing to scan the columns of jobs offered to actors in *The Stage*, and find that the majority were for selling: demonstrations in stores, or by telephone. The confident personalities, good voice projection, and talent for improvisation supposedly instilled by theatre training are useful also in a sales career.

Aidan demonstrated steam irons in department stores on commission for some weeks. As the time dragged by and his sales mounted, I bleakly visualized his tombstone: 'Here lies one who sold 57,000 steam irons'. Then he was on reserve call for this work: if a steam iron demonstrator failed to turn up in any department store in the Home Counties, Aidan was sent there to take over—a Batman for steam irons. He was paid £10 a day if uncalled, for remaining available until 10 a.m.: that is, he stayed in bed till 10 a.m., and had by then clocked up £10. Easy money, it looked to me, taking my first weary coffee break at my desk around that time.

This job led in fact to Aidan's unprecedented 'drying' in public; he is rarely

Demonstrating
steam irons, 1983

23

rendered speechless. Midway through his demonstration in Woolworths in Victoria he caught sight of Conny Heim in the crowd, gazing at him equally open-mouthed. She had arrived from Germany the previous day for a year's teaching in London, and called in to Woollies for teacups and hooks for her new lodgings before ringing Aidan to tell him of her arrival.

He played the piano to accompany contemporary dance classes in London, and was Musical Director for the Lyceum Players' pantomimes in Enfield. He acted as roadie and manager for a friend's unusual act as 'Roger the Robot', who would walk around dance floors interacting with couples. On a Swiss tour with Roger, with attendant language problems, it was particularly difficult to prevent the eager dance hall manager from clearing the floor when Roger was to perform.

In 1982 Aidan worked as a steward at the Apollo Victoria Theatre in London. He took advantage of privileged access to this vast theatre in his first big romance (short-lived), with a girl from the drama course. Telling her only to keep Saturday free, he made arrangements with colleagues at the theatre, and drove Vivienne there at midday. He took her onto the empty stage – and the footlights came on and 'their tune' swelled over all the loudspeakers. He proposed; she accepted; and a tray of champagne, along with the ring, was brought to them by a fellow steward in full evening dress – after which Vivienne was swept off to France for a pre-booked surprise dinner, Aidan having secretly obtained her passport from her parents beforehand.

As steward, he had to wear formal black dress, which he normally kept at the theatre, changing into it on arrival. After one outing with Conny, though, he knew he would barely have time on return to get from Hatfield to London to work. He brought the clothes home the night before, planning to catch the latest possible train to get him to the theatre on time, changing on the train—there would not be time to change on arrival at the theatre. I drove them to the station, with all the sombre black clothing, and got home to find the answerphone winking—Aidan had left his black shoes in his wardrobe. I retrieved them and zoomed back to the station to thrust the shoes through the window of the departing train.

He then found there was no toilet on the crowded train to which he could repair to change costume and, with Conny's assistance and chaperonage, had to change in his seat from crimson jacket and corduroy trousers into the formal black. One fellow-passenger, on leaving the train in London, thanked them for the most entertaining journey he had ever had.

I asked him later why he didn't simply travel in his black steward's clothes. He explained that he felt this would make him conspicuous.

Aidan relished the opportunity his stewardship gave him to smuggle family and friends free into the theatre, though for some of us this treat misfired. My mother, a most respectable member of all other audiences, much disliked being rushed round the foyer and made to dodge behind pillars to avoid the eye of a particularly strict manager. 'I'm quite willing to pay for my ticket', she kept pleading, but that was not the object of the exercise. I arrived early at the stage door for Liza Minnelli's guest artiste evening, bearing beefburger and chips for Aidan from the nearby take-away, and beaker of coffee to drink myself before going into the theatre. Aidan told me to go straight into the auditorium, though, in the wake of a party of guests of the Musical

Director, looking as if I was one of them and sitting in 'a seat that doesn't look as if it's been reserved'. I did not suppose my clasped plastic beaker and book to read on the train enhanced my resemblance to an M.D.'s guest, and did not know quite how to identify an unreserved seat, but obediently did my best. I then had to leave the hot coffee on my seat while I repaired to the ladies' room. Returning, I found a security officer standing by the not-unreserved seat, sternly holding my book and coffee, which I took from him with deep shame, slinking to another seat.

Vivienne was a great fan of John Denver's, and wanted to see his guest appearance at the Apollo. This was on Aidan's day off, so he arranged for a steward-colleague, who had not met Vivienne, to let her into the matinée. By chance, though, Conny called in early that afternoon and asked for Aidan, and the steward rushed her, bewildered, to a seat in the stalls where she had to watch Denver all the afternoon, without much enjoyment. Meanwhile Vivienne waited outside to be summonsed to her free seat, and missed the performance entirely.

Camelot played at the Apollo while Aidan was working there. I learned how little may be known by some performers of the true background to the book of a musical, when I met the young boy playing Tom, whom King Arthur meets before the final battle and sends home to record the events in safety. (Arthur has a splendid line in response to Sir Pellinore's question, 'Who was that, Sire?' —'One of what we all are, Pelly—less than a drop in the great blue ocean of the sunlit sea.' I felt Sir Pellinore should have replied, 'Oh, *him*'.) Enthusiastically I said to the boy, 'Oh, you play Sir Thomas Malory.' 'No', he said, 'I'm Tom of Warwick'. Aidan dragged me away from my attempt to give a lesson on the composition of *Le Morte D'Arthur*.

Aidan then became stage door keeper at the Apollo. Frustrating, off-stage work for him, but bringing some glamour for me. After all others had left the theatre, Aidan had to clear the stage, lock up and leave. Thus, often he would have to remove the gifts thrown by ecstatic fans to visiting stars, who had left them lying. Where should he take them? I became used to finding our dining table in the early morning covered with exotic bouquets, clearing them away to set breakfast. It was a shock, though, to find the fridge, last seen containing only eggs and milk, filled by a huge, highly ornate birthday cake designed for Liza Minnelli.

Aidan had strict instructions for stage-door security, including code-words for dangers to avoid causing general alarm. Once, a suspicious-looking package was left at the stage door. Aidan duly rang the theatre manager and reported, meaningfully, 'Mr Sand is at the stage door'. 'Tell him I'll see him later', came the forgetful reply, and the phone slammed down. Aidan rang again: *'I have Mr Sand at the stage door'*. 'I'm too busy to see him now', snapped the manager, ringing off again. Aidan rang a third time and bawled, sufficient to cause panic throughout the theatre, 'I've got a bloody [euphemism] bomb here, will you come and *do something about it?*'

(This was not Aidan's first experience of the failure of security measures intended to prevent public panic. Working once backstage in our local theatre, he had seen that the staff notice board included the instruction, on discovering a fire, shout ERIF. Experimentally, he shouted, 'ERIF!' several times. No disturbance was caused, among public or staff — no reaction at all, indeed.)

My own deepest humiliation stems from Aidan's stage-door days. Thanks to him

25

I was able to enjoy an evening's performance by Shirley Maclaine. She left afterwards by a side door while fans gathered outside the Apollo stage door eagerly awaiting her, and Aidan cleared the stage and locked up. When I eventually preceded him through the stage door to go home, a groan went up from the crowd, and wails of *'She* doesn't look much like Shirley Maclaine!'. True, I acknowledge—but I have never claimed to, nor ever thought to have this shortcoming proclaimed in the London streets.

In 1984 Aidan worked as disc jockey and compère at two West End clubs, 'Ritzi Park' and 'Bananas'. The second offered 'Special Under-12s Disco Parties' on Saturday afternoons, for which Aidan was dressed alternately as a banana or a gorilla. On the day of a cousin's wedding he was working there, and decided he could not attend the ceremony, but could leave the club after duties at top speed to arrive for the wedding breakfast in a Surrey hotel. I ate my grand meal there nervously watching the door for a breathless banana who had not found time to change.

A tour of Aidan's as disc jockey round London clubs promoting a brand of drinks led me to the first of the many strange venues I have found myself in through my years as a maternal groupie. An early disc-jockeying job was at a small night-club in Ealing. Colin declined the prospective evening's entertainment, but I was eager to see my son's performance. Drawing the line at sitting alone in a night-club, I phoned a friend who lived near Ealing, and asked her to pass an evening with me in this unaccustomed way. She sportingly agreed, and we sat together for two hours, gaudy lights flashing round us, drinking the highly coloured alcoholic concoctions supplied free to Aidan—while we seized the opportunity, yelling above Aidan's blaring disco music, to discuss the overseas membership structure of a society of which we were both officers.

Our elder son, Ian, meanwhile, had developed a passion for Aikido, a Japanese martial art which appeared to need constant practice manipulating long wooden poles – like giant majorette movements. Coming to France with us on holiday, he forbore actually to pack his pole, but purchased a broom handle for his purposes from a hardware shop on arrival. Lungeing and thrusting with a six-foot pole on a crowded camp site or beach could be dangerous; the only safe way Ian could do it was by climbing onto mounds of rock. Thus he would practise Aikido silhouetted against the skyline; every head on the beach would turn. For once, it was our elder son, not our younger, who was entertaining the crowds.

7 An Actor in the House

At last, Aidan having submitted seven contracts and a selection of photographs showing his puppet shows and club work, came the glad day of the arrival of the coveted Equity card. He acquired an agent, and some small professional parts followed, in theatre and film productions as well as in advertisements.

His first professional day's work was in November 1983, as an extra in the veteran Car Rally scene of Limehouse Production's *Winter Sunlight*. As an extra in another film, Aidan was one of many uniformed German soldiers from World War II. This scene was filmed at St Pancras railway station: very early on a Sunday morning, to avoid inconveniencing/alarming more would-be passengers than need be.

In a training film for the General Medical Council, Aidan played a drug addict turning up at a GP's surgery, apparently presenting the symptoms of 'flu, as a lesson in diagnosing drug abuse. For this he was made up over Rice Krispies stuck to his face to simulate pustules for the doctor to detect. Driving home alone, late after filming finished without time to clean up first, he took particular care to avoid giving any cause for the police to stop him, thinking he would have made the worst possible impression and not relishing the prospect of explaining, 'they're just Rice Krispies, officer'.

Aidan's first professional photograph was in a group for Cadbury's chocolate; his first TV commercial was 'An American in England', playing a student, shot in Oxford and Windsor. Taking part in commercials was occasional, highly profitable work. For cream crackers he joined in ritual 'grunging' with the Noddle Grungers of Upper Wallop, illustrating a tale told in voiceover by Kenneth Williams. He swung in a window-cleaner's cradle above Milton Keynes in honour of biscuits; succumbed, swathed in bandages, to the odour from a nurse's armpit for deodorant; was elegantly uniformed on a railway station for corn flakes; donned a Victorian business suit, moustache and top hat to promote office technology; winked in close-up at a school-girl swinging on a football goalpost he was painting. Repeat fees from this last (a chocolate-bar advertisement) were particularly high; we began to speak of our son with the thousand-pound wink. For his first job abroad he was flown to Amsterdam, to be shown on Dutch TV dunking a grapefruit in a teacup, nonplussed, in a futile attempt to make fruit tea – and returned bearing the traditional tulips for his mother.

We have never lost our astonishment at the incomprehension shown by the Department of Social Services as to the freelance life. It seems sometimes that our

A morse code user:
TV advertisement,
1984

27

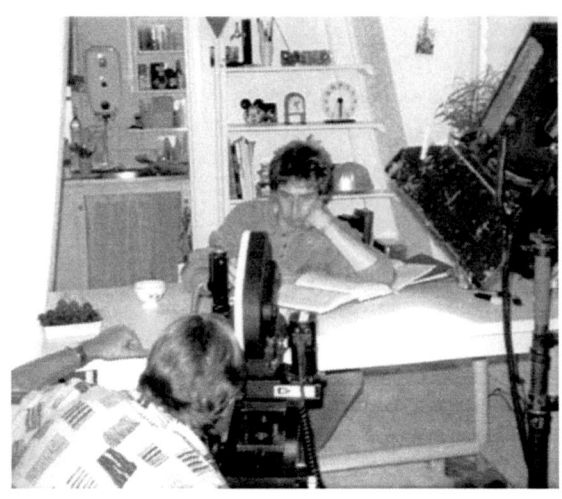

Dunking a grapefruit in a tea-cup to make fruit tea: Dutch TV advertisement, 1985

family must have been the first to work other than fulltime regular hours for a single employer. Actors need unemployment benefit often; but cannot obtain it until they have been out of work for several consecutive weeks, by which time they may have found another short spell of work, and start the cycle again. Aidan had great difficulty persuading the DSS that he had not left the biscuit factory under some terrible cloud, after his two days' swinging above Milton Keynes. 'Why did you only work for them for two days?' the girl kept asking, suspiciously. Car insurance companies, too, regard the acting profession with deep mistrust. Despite years of a clean driving licence, Aidan always had to pay huge insurance premiums, on account of his profession: 'you might give a lift to Michael Caine, and we might have to pay for an operation for him', he was constantly assured.

Most of Aidan's jobs were so short-lasting and far-away that we rarely knew where, at what, even whether he was working, though he was still living at home. The late end to the theatre or cinematic day, the distances to travel, and Aidan's inclination to nocturnal life and an undisturbed house all meant that he went to bed in the small hours, long after us, and slept well into the day. Colin, indeed, having departed for work himself every morning well before Aidan rose, rarely encountered his housemate. I have read that nocturnal animals are naturally scheduled to allow dual habitation of the earth by non-mingling sets of species. This system seems equally to allow two non-meeting generations of different tastes and habits to share a single residence without clashing, especially when one works in the theatre world.

Although having become Equity-qualified for professional work, and obtaining much, Aidan kept a 'day job' for sustenance between stage work. He worked occasionally as stage crew at the Forum Theatre in Hatfield and Campus West in Welwyn Garden City. The latter complex included a cinema where he was sometimes projectionist ('currently appearing' there, as the local paper, writing of his career,

**Simple Simon,
Hampstead, 1984-85**

tactfully put it). One Hallowe'en he borrowed a green light filter, smoke machine and mask and set them up in our hall. When he heard trick-or-treaters coming to the door, he switched on the light and smoke, and leered at the startled little witches and wizards, cackling through a green haze.

He also helped with the redecoration of the whole theatre complex. 'Where do you think all the old carpet is now?' a friend of Diana's wondered, as they walked through the newly furbished foyer. 'Well, some of it's on my parents' bedroom floor', Diana was able to tell her.

Aidan extended his interests to filming, making a horror video at home and around—a very noisy business, involving many shrieking students from East Herts College and much false blood—and a 40-minute film about the college, *Think Yourself In,* which was used to promote it.

Then came panto. His first major professional role was in 1984 as Simple Simon in *Dick Whittington* at Islington Town Hall Theatre, then the New End Theatre, Hampstead. I took a carful of women friends to lunch and a matinée—not quite the usual ladies-who-lunch type of excursion. Aidan stole the reviews—'He leads the rest of the cast by the nose', commented the *Ham and High*; the producer went bankrupt. Aidan's career was off to a prophetic start.

And television. He then appeared as a grubby, greasy, black-vested keyboard player in *The Two Ronnies*—not a pretty sight— in *Tripods*, and as a bomber pilot on Thames TV.

In 1985 Aidan changed his agent. Ian also had an agent, for software sales. Both were young women with husky voices, and, coincidentally, the same Christian name. Both would telephone and murmur effusively, '*Hallo*, Mrs Bell, it's Josie'. I would have to wait for further data before working out which of my sons' careers was in question, not liking to indicate that I did not know.

For the 1985-6 season Aidan again appeared in pantomime, *Mother Goose* at

29

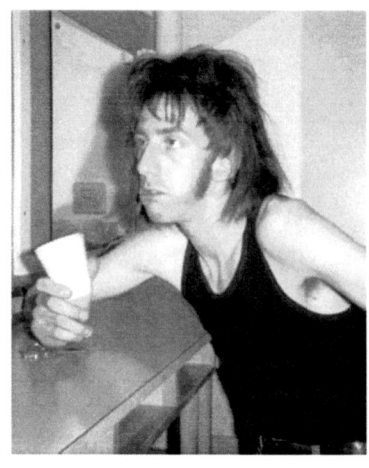

A keyboard player in *The Two Ronnies*, 1985

Bristol Old Vic, as Mike the Milkman, with Martin Clunes as Herbert and Samantha Bond as principal boy. Mother Goose herself was played by the late, charming Harold Innocent. We met him backstage; he was delighted to find that his huge, ginger Dame's wig had been placed on the floor outside his dressing room, with a saucer of milk.

Certain responsibilities accrue to theatre motherhood. The mothers of medical practitioners do not feel obliged to hover approvingly during treatment of patients; those of business managers to sit beside the desk cheering on their dealings; teachers' mothers to nod wisely at the back of classes. Public performance by one's young, though, demands maternal attendance at least once. I read how Rachel Kempson, (stage) mother of Vanessa, Lynn and Corin Redgrave, made a point of seeing all their

Mike the Milkman in *Mother Goose*; Bristol Old Vic, 1985-86

shows, whichever side of the Atlantic. Well, she could afford it ...

As Aidan's devoted follower I attended many shows I would not normally have chosen to see. One such was *Aladdin* starring Stanley Baxter—Aidan's third pantomime. Baxter played pantomime each year, alternately in Edinburgh or Glasgow. At the end of 1986 we drove the near-400 miles to Glasgow to see his show. We found his thick Scottish brogue incomprehensible, and frequently puzzled to work out what he had said; then, wincing, wished we hadn't. The presence of so many bewildered, exhausted small children at this decidedly adult-blue, late-night performance seemed inexplicable.

One of Aidan's parts was that of the executioner who does not after all cut off Aladdin's head. He and his fellow Oriental officer wore costumes of such elaborate and heavy fabric that they could not sit down in them, and were paid extra for this inconvenience. Actors' pay in this instance varied, not according to the length of their parts or intensity of the emotions portrayed, but with the thickness of their costume.

Aidan played several parts in a Manchester Library Theatre production of *A Funny Thing Happened on the Way to the Forum,* with Patrick Barlow as Pseudolus. The men wore togas, and seemed to me to extend their comic playing to use of their exposed legs, posturing as they cannot in limb-concealing trousers; an added dimension for male comedy. He played again with that Company as Hank in *Huckleberry Finn —* after the years with the Hertford Symphony Orchestra, now striving to learn the banjo.

*A Funny Thing Happened on the Way to the Forum***, 1988**

31

8 Touring the Country

Aidan toured in several productions, playing usually a week in each town visited, having to find digs locally to live in for the period. His first tour was in a children's show, *James and the Giant Peach*, based on the story by Roald Dahl. Tall and thin, Aidan auditioned for the role of the grasshopper, but was in fact cast as orphan James's wicked Aunt Spiker. Six feet tall, thin indeed, built up with high shoes and beehive wig—'a marvellously angular Aunt Spiker,' *The Stage* called him— Aidan made a towering and intimidating contrast to Aunt Sponge, played by Lewis Barber, short and plump, rendered rotund by a cushioned costume. Aidan sang some stunningly high notes in this role, beginning to realize how very wide was the range of his voice.

While this show was playing in Manchester, the two aunts and James were invited to appear on a Saturday breakfast-time children's television programme starting at 7 am, *The Wide-Awake Club*. Child actors have to be duplicated for long theatre runs, so there was a spare James available in London; but Aidan and Lewis as the aunts would have to drive from Manchester to London after the Friday night show, sleep for any remaining hours of the night in a hotel, report early to the studio, dress and make up, sing, and drive rapidly back to Manchester for the afternoon matinée.

I was at a conference in a college that weekend, but determined to see Aidan's TV appearance. I rose early on the Saturday and switched on the television in the common room, where a collection of books with award-winning indexes was on

Aidan as Aunt Spiker in *James and the Giant Peach*, **with his real-life sister, 1988**

display. I did not know that I had in fact already missed the *James and the Giant Peach* item, which was put on as almost the first, to allow the guests' prompt departure northwards. I kept the programme on for the rest of its length, watching hopefully for my son. Batman, sport, puppets and cartoon figures appeared on screen, to the astonishment of my fellow conference delegates, visiting the indexes exhibition after breakfast.

Aidan commuted from Hatfield to this show at many of its venues, even Canterbury. On a matinée day there, when Colin was to drive Diana early to Heathrow to fly off for a holiday, they woke Aidan at six am when they left, as arranged, so he too could make an early departure. I rose around eight to, I thought, an empty house, later going to open Aidan's curtains. He was still in bed, having fallen asleep again. I had to wake him with the charged words, 'it's nine o'clock, and you're due on stage in Canterbury at two'.

The two wicked aunts in Roald Dahl's story meet their well-merited end when the giant peach rolls over them and squashes them. On the last performance of the *James* tour, as the deadly fruit advanced towards them, Aidan turned to his fellow aunt and whispered, as Henry Gibson did to his fellow Nazi at the end of the film, *Blues Brothers*, as their car hurtles into space off an unfinished bridge, 'I've always loved you'.

Next came a tour of *Joseph and the Amazing Technicolour Dreamcoat* (a show Aidan had earlier starred in at the X Theatre in our garage, where it had a cast of four). He played brother Asher, and sustained two injuries in the course of the tour. The first was when the brothers kill a goat to soak Joseph's coat in its blood. The goat was made of wood, and the boys would crowd round to dismantle it. One night a brother swung a piece back into Aidan's face, causing bleeding. The accident book for the theatre duly recorded, 'Mr Bell injured by the goat. Blood drawn'. Later, unofficially rehearsing one of his own compositions with a brother singer, he fell heavily against the piano and to the floor, badly straining his back. He could not claim compensation as he should not have been in the piano room. For the rest of that performance, Joseph had only ten brothers; particularly difficult when the bags of corn were being given out, then searched one by one for the missing gold cup. Aidan insisted on playing the following night—stiffly—as it was the performance for which a party of family and friends was driving to see the show at that theatre, in Harlow, the nearest to home on the tour. The next day he was actually given sick leave. This was also the one day's rest for the cast on the whole tour.

On the tenth anniversary of the tour, *Joseph* played in Liverpool, with a 20-piece band—the only week it enjoyed this splendour. Unfortunately there was a power failure in the theatre one night that week, and the performance started 40 minutes late with the mike-less singers having to project over the unplugged band.

Aidan was usually appointed Equity Deputy for the companies he played in, representing the troupe in dealings with management. He also seemed to take on the responsibility for finding accommodation for them where they played on tours. He was developing personnel management skills on the side, too; even being called out at night sometimes when actor friends threatened suicide.

Aidan's last role in England before he left for a Continental tour was in a David

33

The Ideal Gnome Expedition, **1989**

Wood children's theatre production, a matinées-only show for the very young, *The Ideal Gnome Expedition* [*sic*]. Aidan played two villains: Whacker, a road-mending hydraulic tool that constantly jumped up and down; and a brutally stupid guard dog—'My ears are specially trained not to listen'. Pondering the philosophical implications of this helped to pass the trivial plot for me. This show's tour included playing at Sadler's Wells in December 1989. I attended an Editorial Board meeting at a London Institution one morning, followed by a working lunch; then off to Sadler's Wells to witness the gnomes' adventures.

Aidan had to deliver all Securidog's threats and snarls in a low growl. As a result of weeks of this, the worst happened—he developed a nodule on his vocal chords, due to 'abuse' of his voice. Luckily the voice recovered on abandoning that register, and was subsequently found not to be 'abused' by use in the highest register when he came to sing falsetto frequently.

I managed to see every show of Aidan's in the UK at one venue at least, and sometimes would stay on in pleasant places for a short holiday. I set off with him to the Isle of Wight for a summer week with the *Ideal Gnomes*. At the ferry port, Aidan found that his car could not get a place in time for him to arrive for his matinée, and decided to go at once as a pedestrian passenger on the departing boat. Attracting much attention by calling loudly for me to find his make-up, he left me with the huge, unfamiliar, laden car to take across the ferry and the Island—a holiday baptism of fire.

On tour, of course, Aidan was usually away from home; but whenever the current show was playing near enough for him to sleep at home and drive to the theatre he would extend hospitality (and petrol costs share) to friends in the company. Thus we usually had either no resident son, or three or four bundles in sleeping bags scattered round the house after midnight.

9 Priming the Piper

Following the productions of *Piper* in 1982 and 1984, East Herts College performed scenes from it in the Welwyn Garden City Youth Drama festival in May 1986; but still it had found no commercial backer. In September that year Aidan hired a recording studio in Milton Keynes for six days to produce a demo cassette of *Piper*, driving off there for some very happy days with musical colleagues. Colm Wilkinson, who had been so friendly during the tour of *Jesus Christ Superstar*, would have sung the role of the Mayor, but was committed to *Les Misérables*. The children of Hamelin were recruited from stage schools, a minibus and driver hired to take them from London to Milton Keynes and back, with Diana the Nursery Nurse in charge.

Aidan exulted in directing the recording, and determined to make this a part of his career. Many demo cassettes of *Piper* were produced and distributed, but they brought him no reward but praise.

Then an influx of unexpected funds into the family coffers occurred. Ian, while reading maths at Cambridge University, had written another computer game, together with fellow student David Braben. They did this for relaxation during their second university year; then sold the game, 'Elite', to a software company, BBC's Acornsoft, and settled to concentrate on their studies in their third year, both indeed achieving good degrees.

Meanwhile, 'Elite' took off. It was launched in September 1984, Acornsoft hiring Thorpe Park in Surrey, where the world's first underground roller-coaster ride had just opened, for the occasion: as Francis Spufford wrote later, 'in 1984, computer games did not have launch parties ... The reviews of the game were rapturous'.* It became a cult, making sales in the Acornsoft version of almost 150,000: as there were only 150,000 or so BBC Micros in the world at that point, it was total market saturation, according to Spufford. When the contract with Acornsoft expired, interest in the other rights was so intense that the boys' newly-acquired agent was able to hold an auction – the first software auction, and shown on *Channel 4 News*. Less fame-hungry than his brother, Ian resented having to take a day away from his studies for the shooting of this programme, shortly before his final university exams.

Subsequently 'Elite' was adapted for many types of computers, including the Nintendo Entertainment System and the early PC. It was critically acclaimed as the grandmaster of its genre, and 'proliferated across the world'. Its young authors were awarded the first ever gold floppy disc. Eventually it became, as Spufford put it, 'a landmark in the history of computer games'.

I began to enjoy a degree of trans-generational fame, as friends reported their young sons gazing at them in unaccustomed awe to exclaim, '*You mean you know the mother of the boy who wrote "Elite"?*'

Royalties rolled in, hugely. Ian moved up several income brackets, far above his

---

* *Backroom Boys* by Francis Spufford; Faber and Faber, 2003

Acornsoft BBC Elite box

parents. Indeed, Colin, in employment as a research scientist himself ever since leaving Oxford, totalled his annual earnings in that respectable capacity, and found that his elder son had exceeded them, sum for sum, before graduating.

Fortunately, both Ian and David much enjoyed and admired Aidan's music. They decided to put their money where their ears were, and back a showcase production of *Piper*. A Limited Company was set up in November 1986 for theatre production, with investment from the 'Elite' proceeds. Aidan was Co-Director with a music agent from Welwyn Garden City; Diana became Company Secretary; and the name was that used by Conny and her brother for their occasional enterprises: Pink Hippo Productions Limited.

This name began to loom large in my life, as Company stationery of all kinds was printed, giving our address and telephone number. At last Pink Hippo acquired its own telephone line, in Aidan's room, with extension in Secretary Diana's room. The Company was listed in local telephone directories and in the local classified directories, under THEATRICAL COSTUMES, EQUIPMENT AND SUPPLIES. This caused much nuisance for us, as customers continually rang to ask for costumes for concerts and parties. Around Hallowe'en and Christmas requests for costumes seemed ceaseless. We began to wonder if we were in the wrong businesses: what the people wanted clearly was fancy dress rather than any of the various services tendered on our answerphone.

Diana demanded of the directory publishers that Pink Hippo be removed from the costume hire column. Two editions later, they responded. Our bungalow then appeared instead as the fourth of five entries entry in the column for all West Hertfordshire, THEATRES AND CONCERT HALLS.

We did not know it, but another Pink Hippo Company was formed at around the same time, producing videos, with London office premises. There were extraordinary similarities: both companies had chosen that name because of a present from a girl friend; both had their logo designed by an artistic friend, both logos showing a large pink hippo seen from behind, grinning backwards over its vast pink shoulder. (Eventually the larger, metropolitan animal outlived the provincial calf.)

Piper was produced at Campus West Theatre, Welwyn Garden City, in October 1987, with a host of producers invited, and a hospitality suite booked for them. It was very much a family enterprise, with Aidan singing the role of the Mayor ('without question he was the star of the show ... it was magnificent', wrote the local paper) as well as composing and producing the whole; Ian (and David)'s money funding it; and Diana acting as wardrobe mistress, secretary, production assistant, and chaperone. This last was essential for the production, with all the Hamelin children (from a local dancing school) needed to dance on stage and follow the Piper off in procession. Luckily, Diana, after attending a two-year Nursery Nursing course, had gained her NNEB qualification, which enabled her to obtain a child chaperone's licence – so extremely convenient for Pink Hippo!

Involvement in the *Piper* production also sparked off some dramatic ambition in Diana, and she asked to appear on stage too. The Director objected that the place of the chaperone was with the children, not behind the footlights; Diana argued, irrefutably, that if the children were all on stage, and she also, then she was indeed

Piper, Welwyn Garden City, 1987; Paul Smith, Claire Fowler and Aidan

with the children. As wardrobe mistress, she provided herself with a costume; as Company Secretary, she authorized her participation in the performance; and as child chaperone (a most ineffectual one, in terms of the tale!) she accompanied the children onto the stage and off into oblivion.

Conny and a friend from Germany came to England that week, intending to see the sights and shows of London. They managed just one day in town; hands were too badly needed for *Piper* for them to be allowed to leave Hertfordshire again.

My own role was to be gracious hostess to the impresario guests. However, only two producers accepted the invitation, and one of those rang on the day to say that his chauffeur was ill so it was impossible for him to attend (well, of course). We never spotted the other to expend all my graciousness on.

We had discovered Piper-Heidseik Champagne around this time, hoarded a supply against the glad day of such a production, and now exultantly celebrated with it.

However, the show lost money profusely: as a younger brother, Aidan was an effective tax loss. Plans for a tour of *Piper*, and a showcase production of *On Location*, did not come to fruition.

Piper has indeed proved a most effective money-loser through the years, and in a wide spread of places. Conny, studying drama at Freiburg University, in southern Germany, translated it into German and produced a two-week showcase run, in October 1988. Rudolf Kostas, a professional opera singer, was persuaded to sing the part of the narrator. The show was marvellous; large debts were incurred.

We all went out to Freiburg to see this production; Aidan's career was greatly extending our travel experience. Diana went for the first week, with her boyfriend, Andrew. They arrived on the day of the first performance, knowing that all concerned would be at the dress rehearsal, and they were to go straight to join them. Unfortunately they lost the paper with the venue address, and no information centre seemed to have heard of *Piper*. They stood in the centre of Freiburg, quite at a loss, when, as if a ray had shone down from the clouds directing their gaze, Diana saw a poster for *Piper*. They crossed exultantly to it, their English cries of delight drawing the attention of a passing Fräulein who—strong coincidence—was a friend of Conny's, and stopped to urge them to see the show, telling them, in English, how good it was. Yes, said Diana, she knew; she was the composer's sister. Understandably, the girl looked disbelieving, until Diana opened her jacket to reveal a tee-shirt with the flying Piper logo, matching the poster; upon which she and Andrew were personally escorted to the rehearsal.

Colin's and my own difficulties in reaching the show, a week later, were different. We flew to Basel, border town with its airport in France, shops in Switzerland, and railway station in Germany, where Colin asked for two railway tickets to Freiburg. Because of his faulty accent, though, he was given tickets for Fribourg in Switzerland instead. We did not notice this, and boarded the right train for our destination.

An inspector came through the train, and was greatly agitated at the sight of our tickets, speaking at length to us in incomprehensible German. When he found a bilingual colleague who explained the problem to us, we somewhat smugly felt that as we were indeed on the train taking us where we wished to go, the discrepancy was their problem, not ours. However, Nemesis struck: they insisted that we pay them immediately for tickets to Freiburg, and could apply for reimbursement for the unused tickets to Fribourg on returning to Basel the following week. An inauspicious start to an already financially strained holiday, and typical side-effect of an Aidan Bell production.

Freiburg proved wholly charming, though: a 12th-century town, perfectly preserved, with rare twin-spired cathedral. Along the high street each shop had its trade mark laid in the paving-stone outside: diamonds before the jeweller's, spectacles before the oculist's, a lamb before the butcher's. Astonishingly, each shop still occupied the correctly signalled premises, none having changed trade or moved away through all the years.

Later, Conny and Aidan nearly found a backer to produce *Piper* again in Germany. At the second meeting to discuss the project, though, they were told, sadly, that the company had sustained severe financial losses and could no longer contemplate mounting *Piper*. Even the mere idea of putting on this show apparently entails bankruptcy...

On holiday in Hamelin, Conny and Aidan approached the Director of the Hamelin theatre and offered him *Piper* to produce. He declared himself interested but unable to produce the work, and asked for a copy of the score to deposit in Hamelin Museum. From manuscript to museum, *sans* professional performance—the mark of a true master, surely.

39

10 Musical Muster

Aidan and Brian wrote four musicals together, becoming designated, of course, the Rice and Lloyd Webber of East Herts: *Piper*, *Aesop*, *Card in a Window*, and *Elite*. The last was based on Ian and David's computer game—the first musical to be based on one, including songs, 'Assassin's Touch', 'Just a Game', 'A Contract is a Contract' and 'I Am Elite'. Demo recordings were made of them all, at home or in rented studios.

Aidan's bedroom gradually filled with instruments and recording equipment; the piano was succeeded by an electronic keyboard. Singing friends from college and co-performers from shows Aidan was in came to take parts in the recordings. Concerned about the constant noise floating out—especially as the thermal combination of electronic instruments, several players and singers packed into a small room, and sustained effort, necessitated wide-open windows—we changed the rooms of 'Carillon' round so that Aidan's activities occurred at the back of the house, sound wafting out towards the school playing field behind, rather than to our normally quiet residential road.

For the first *Elite* recording tryout it was all voices to the mike. Diana was then in her early teens, and her English missy voice piped oddly through the raunchy chorus of market traders in 'Sniff of Exotic', enunciating carefully,

Hemp, Mould and Opium,
Flash-stash stored to the optimum;
Sex, pain, orgasmabox,
Pleasure pads serving lusto-studshoks;
Come buy, get laid, get high,
If not, disappear.

One evening Aidan and Brian asked me not to come into the room while they were actually recording. There was a phone call for Brian; I listened outside the door, heard that they were indeed recording, and did not go in. Later, when I told him he had had a call, Brian asked me what time it had been. It was in fact just when there was a space-ship announcement,

'All personnel are reminded that sexual contact with feline-orientated aliens should not take place while on duty.'

Trying to remember what I'd heard through the closed door, I said 'It was when you got to something like, don't have intercourse with cats while the train is at the station'.

Later, at the railway station waiting for his train home, hearing an announcement over the Tannoy, Brian was convulsed.

For the recording of *Aesop*, with its many characters, Aidan wanted a different singer for each, and brought in colleagues from college and from his various touring shows, using family members too. Diana was the mouse who gnawed through the lion's net; I narrated the story of the fox and the crow.

40

Card in a Window was a one-woman show about a girl from the north who comes to London, fails to make a living in various respectable ways, and finally advertises her personal services. Walking through London at this time with Brian or Aidan proved embarrassing, as they would dart into every telephone booth they passed to grab the cards for inspiration and authentication. The inevitable happened; Brian's briefcase spilled open while he was coaching a group of young actors; the cards were enthusiastically collected and presented to him as he blushingly explained they were for his musical research—*really*.

Music composition brought Aidan conspicuous and flattering billing, though, par for the course, little income. He wrote background music for 'Elite' the game; but for the landing on one planet a four-bar phrase from 'The Blue Danube' was used, in deliberate echo of the film, *2001*. The printed credits then read, jointly (and in alphabetical order): 'Music by Aidan Bell and Johann Strauss'.

Ian Harrold, Aidan's former school music teacher, who had been the Musical Director for the 1987 *Piper* production, was Associate Conductor of the Hertford Symphony Orchestra, and adapted scores for them. He arranged a suite of some of the themes from *Piper*, for solo cello and orchestra, which they performed occasionally. Aidan wanted to record a performance, but the sight of the technical equipment with booms and dangling microphones caused much concern to the musicians, and it took all the charm of the conductor, Iain Sutherland, to persuade them to play to them.

The Hertford Symphony Orchestra played 'Dances from *Piper*' at a children's concert at Castle Hall, Hertford, in 1988. There were four items, by Handel, Mozart, Tchaikovsky, and Aidan, all receiving equal billing on the posters. After the *Piper* suite, Sutherland brought Aidan to the rostrum to take a bow; then, 'And so, on to Tchaikovsky', he announced. It seemed an accolade indeed.

Aidan's personality well fitted his calling, and in private life too he was able to coast a great deal on charm. Like the Queen, he rarely carried money, though for the opposite reason—sheer lack of it; but the river of life would open before him to make way. Once when he had persuaded a photocopy shop to produce a batch of programmes for him in much less than a reasonable time, he phoned me from miles away when collection was due—he couldn't possibly get there, could I drive over to Cheshunt . . . ? Losing two hours' working time to get to the shop, I found it galling to see the girl's face fall as I asked to collect 'the programmes you are doing for Aidan Bell'. Mothers of his friends, too, seemed very prone to succumb to his appeal, and many a time, on hearing, 'Oh, he's just like a son to me!', I would grit my teeth to refrain from growling, 'Back off, lady, he *has* a mother'.

Elite (the musical) was thought to stand a better chance of promotion in the US than at home, and Aidan seized the offer of a producer-friend's going there to take tapes of it over. This meant making a really good recording: Aidan hired a studio deep in Berkshire and persuaded professional friends to turn up and record for him (all free: all his recordings were produced on shoestrings). The session would have to take place from midnight on a Saturday night, when the studio and singers were available, and just before the departure for US. The date proved, in fact, to be that of the last night in London of *Chess*, for which Aidan had bought three hugely expensive tickets months before with high anticipation of a splendid occasion. The tickets were for

41

himself, me, and Stephen Keeling, Musical Director of the Manchester Library Theatre productions Aidan had been in, who had come south to live with us while seeking work in London. (Just a party of three: musicals were not to the taste of Aidan's father, a devotee of classical music.)

Come the longed-for date of the last night all was frantic activity setting up the recording session by a succession of phone calls. Late in the afternoon the studio owner rang to cancel the booking; Aidan, near desperation, persuaded him to allow the session to go ahead, but had to agree to pay in cash for the studio hire that night—no cheque or card payment. The banks, of course, were now closed for the weekend, and we did not have sufficient cash in hand to meet the studio hire fee; let alone the complication of Aidan's being uncertain how much money there was currently in the Pink Hippo account. Colin had already drawn half the daily allowance from our personal account that morning, so I could draw only a limited amount from that one. I went to our local cash point armed with both my card and Aidan's to see what total of notes I could amass: as so often, it was out of order. We agreed to stop at a cash point on the drive down to London; dressed for the *Chess* performance; and finally set off.

We found no working cash point all the way to London, and arrived at the theatre with no time to eat first, and moreover having to purchase a bottle of champagne suggested by the lead singer for *Elite*, Peter Straker. While Aidan went to buy this, persuading the merchant to keep the bottle in his fridge until we collected it after the show, I bought packets of sandwiches to serve for us instead of dinner—but our expensive seats proved so conspicuous in the elegantly dressed audience at the Prince Edward Theatre that we could not bring ourselves to eat them.

As the show ended, Aidan, who had anticipated with such excitemen the last night of *Chess*, was worrying about getting to the studio on time, fidgeting to be gone, and willing speeches and encores to be curtailed. At last we left, and lost some time searching for the wine shop with our bottle of champagne kept cool. Then we drove to Oxford Street, where I could use my cash card to enter a bank and attempt to draw the needed notes with both my card and Aidan's, increasing my large loan to Pink Hippo. (I had always known that mothers were supposed to function as ministering angels, but not expected also to have to be a financial theatre one.) Aidan could not park near the bank, so had to drop me, clutching both our cash cards, and drive off to find a parking space, keeping Stephen with him to come back for me when they knew in which direction I should make for the car.

I played both cards at the cash point and succeeded in obtaining sufficient notes, which I crammed into my evening bag. I left the bank and walked along Oxford Street trying hard to look as if I knew just where I was making for, would be meeting someone immediately, and was not clasping a large number of high-currency notes in my glittering little bag. Rarely have I been so glad to see anyone as Stephen when he loped up to lead me to Aidan's car. I was then driven to King's Cross to make my midnight way home alone by train, while the boys set off for their late-night Berkshire recording session, complete with champers and loadsamoney.

11 Comrades in Arts

While playing in *A Funny Thing Happened on the Way to the Forum* near Manchester, in 1988, Aidan agreed to drive Stephen Keeling down after one Saturday night show, to stay with us overnight and travel by train to London the next morning, where he was to play the organ at a friend's wedding. (An appropriate task for Stephen, who looked like a rather older version of the cherubic young figure of Folly in Bronzino's picture, 'Allegory of Time', with tumbled curls.) All was arranged: Stephen would walk to Hatfield railway station after breakfast, leaving Aidan to sleep off the three-hours' post-midnight drive.

Stephen woke, though, to the realization that he had left his sheet music in Manchester, and could not play the required pieces without it. We started to ring musical friends locally who might have them (pre-Internet days, those); but those who would have such religious music were, at that hour on a Sunday morning, in church, not answering their telephones. At last, though, Ian Harrold proved to have one piece; the other was the Bach/Gounod 'Ave Maria' with Gounod's voice setting of the prayer superimposed over Bach's Prelude no. 1 from 'The Well-tempered Clavier'. Ian had the Bach Prelude, and undertook to transcribe and superimpose the Gounod part from memory while Aidan drove Stephen the nine miles from Hatfield to Ian's Stevenage home to collect the music.

They arrived, to have the door opened by an old lady who had never heard of Ian Harrold. The honest natures and despair of the boys were so apparent that she let them into her flat to telephone Ian, who turned out to live at the next number up in that road, but round a corner, so that he and she had never met. They collected the music, but found that after all the delays Stephen had missed his London train. Aidan had to forgo all thoughts of catching up on sleep to get him to the church (in Ealing) on time.

Stephen was asked to play the piano for the after-show party on the first night of the 1989 London production of Stephen Sondheim's *A Little Night Music* at the Piccadilly Theatre. Tunes by Sondheim were specified for him to play, and we heard 24-hour daily Sondheim music practice on our piano, it seemed, from the booking to the date. As Aidan would be playing too far away on tour that night to manage to attend even the party – to his great frustration – I got to attend this splendid event with Stephen. Having dressed up for the occasion to the most glamorous extent my wardrobe permitted, I was embarrassed when the usual constraints of time and money affecting all visits to the theatre with Aidan and his like compelled us to eat in a McDonalds before going into the theatre.

From our privileged seats in the front row of the circle, though, Stephen saw but little of the show, as there sat in the front of the stalls a man who, judging solely by the back of his head and his position in the audience, might be Sondheim himself. Terrified at the idea of playing the composer's own music before him at the party, Stephen gazed unremittingly at this man throughout the show, waiting for him to turn his profile and be identified. It proved a false alarm, though, and at the party, unattended by Sondheim, Stephen played proficiently. While he waited nervously to

43

start playing, I, so far from my accustomed milieu, leaned maternally over the piano making soothing sounds; and was taken aback to be asked by a guest, 'what do you do?' She had taken me for a singer warming up for performance.

As he too was composing a musical, *Maddie* (later retitled *The Time of My Life*). Stephen was allotted the piano in our living room to work on, while Aidan used the keyboard in his bedroom. Thus, according to where in the house I worked myself on indexing – in Ian's old room where my computer was, or on the dining table where I could spread out papers – I had a choice between listening to the emerging *Maddie* or *Card in a Window*. Or, when two other friends came to join Aidan and Stephen to rehearse their proposed quartet cabaret act, I had live, loud music while I worked.

Stephen Keeling was one of the students at the Stephen Sondheim Musical Workshop in Oxford in 1989, the first course following the installation of the Cameron Mackintosh Chair of Contemporary Theatre. In fact he was the thirteenth student in what was to have been a class of twelve. He heard of the application opportunity late (it was originally intended for Oxford students only, but later extended to external applicants), and after working many hours on his presentation, when it was still incomplete, he phoned to ask if he could bring it to Oxford himself on the Sunday after the Friday deadline. They agreed; he worked continuously, made the long train journey from Hatfield, and delivered his score and supplementary letters. Then a letter arrived stating that his application had been too late (and had indeed been forwarded from Oxford to Mackintosh's London office —which would have been so much easier for Stephen to deliver to directly himself). Total gloom and bitterness prevailed.

Then, just before Christmas, we found Cameron Mackintosh himself on our answerphone, saying that he and Sondheim had been so pleased by Stephen K.'s work that they were making a thirteenth place on the course for him; he was to ring Mackintosh's secretary after Christmas. More champagne, and exultation unconfined—until the phone call to the secretary met with blank assertions that the twelve places were filled, the class was closed. Stephen persuaded the secretary to check with Mackintosh, who had informed him, but not her, of the extra place. I was meanwhile worrying about the finances, remembering the students from East Herts who had been unable to take up their Drama Schools places because of the cost; I wondered whether there would be high fees to be paid, and if Stephen could apply anywhere for a grant. 'Ask her about costs!' I hissed, when finally his place was assured over the phone. To Stephen's diffident enquiry, 'Is there any money involved?' the secretary replied in shocked tones, 'We're not going to *pay* you to come!'.

In fact the course was most generously sponsored, records and volumes relevant to Sondheim's work being supplied free to all the students, as well as pairs of complimentary tickets to Mackintosh's shows running in London, so that the students could observe and criticize these. As Aidan was still away on tour, I was again the lucky one to accompany Stephen to all these splendid shows, sweeping with him past the long queues outside to take my place in the aisle seat, fifth row from the front, seeing, in less than three weeks, *Les Miserables, The Phantom of the Opera*, and *Sunday in the Park with George*.

Stephen thoroughly enjoyed the course, which was most enlighteningly tutored by Sondheim, who oversaw the composition of a musical by each of its members (in Stephen K.'s case, *Maddie)*. We ironically recalled his terrified gazing at the back of the pseudo-Sondheim's head during *A Little Night Music* only weeks before, little knowing how soon he was to find Sondheim a most congenial colleague.

The second production mounted by Pink Hippo Productions (following *Piper*) was another showcase production, of a musical composed by Keeling, *The Devil and Mr Stone*. This was based on a morality tale by the American poet, Stephen Vincent Benét; a version of the Faust legend centring on money. Auditions were advertised in *The Stage* and held in London at Pineapple Studios. Nikki Ankara, narrator on the tour of *Joseph and the Amazing Technicolour Dreamcoat*, for whom Brian and Aidan had written *Card in a Window*, was cast as the heroine, making her London debut. It was performed three times at the Donmar Warehouse in July 1989, at 11 p.m. *(sic)* on Saturday and Sunday, and on Sunday afternoon. This was both because the theatre was cheapest to book at those times, and the cast were mostly appearing in paid runs, free for the Donmar only after Saturday curtain-down.

Aidan was the producer; Stephen was Musical Director; Alan Pope, the stage manager of Welwyn Garden City's Campus West, designed the lighting. Diana, again, was unpaid production assistant. After the hero concluded Act I by grandiosely scattering coins all over the ground, the interval then saw Diana on the uncurtained stage painstakingly gathering them up. (Perhaps one day Diana may come to write 'A Stage Sister's Story'?)

Harold Innocent came to see this performance, sitting at the end of the front row beside the piano, played by. A smoke machine was on the piano, and as Jabez Stone made his dread descent to Hell, Stephen pressed this to fill the stage with black smoke. The machine was slightly mis-angled, though, and poor Harold instead was engulfed in the fumes of the underworld.

At the age of 25, Aidan claimed on the strength of this production to be the youngest producer in the West End.

The lyrics for *The Devil and Mr Stone* were by Dennis Pickford, who stayed with us in Hatfield for its run. He was a 6'7" tall bass singer, much in demand for the role of Goliath—and thus quite exposed to greetings by fans in the streets, as there was no difficulty in identifying him, or possibility of disguise by singlasses and a turned-up coat collar. Aidan seized the opportunity to have him record the role of the lion in *Aesop*, roaring magnificently, counterbalanced by Diana's piping mouse.

Nikki Ankara, pretty, young and blonde, was later cast in the disastrous 'people's musical', *Bernadette*, to play Bernadette's mother, stooping unrecognizably under a black shawl. She then went into *Miss Saigon*, playing a caged prostitute in Bangkok and understudying Ellen, the hero's American wife. Reporting for work each evening, she would not know which of these very different women she was to portray. Taking over on one occasion as Ellen, she sang for the first time with yet another replacement for Tam, Miss Saigon's supposedly two-year-old son, actually played by a succession of five-year-olds of either sex. A through professional, the tot (on this occasion a small girl) allowed Nikki to clasp her close through the final death scene. As the curtain closed, she looked up and asked politely, 'Who are you?'

45

12 The Professional Stage Mother

I experienced another side of maternal theatre life as a result of daughter Diana's second career. She had found the theatre whirl of working on *Piper* so stimulating, in contrast to the solitude of nannying, that the production changed her life; she turned to work in theatre management. She began by working as a leisure centre usherette ('not much different from nannying — you have to make them hang their coats up and behave properly') and in box offices locally; and made use of the Matron's Licence she had first acquired to supervise those wandering children of Hamelin to work as a professional child chaperone.

Any child working in the public entertainment or media industry, performing or modelling, must at all times, including during rehearsals and auditions, be supervised by an adult who is solely responsible for the child's welfare.

Years later, Diana was asked to write about child chaperonage for a book on child models and actors.* She provided this account:

> A large percentage of chaperones are the child's parents, especially for modelling or acting babies and toddlers. Baby shoots may consist of mums and babies sitting around gossiping like any church hall toddler group. At this stage most mothers are doing this for their own pleasure rather than to help the child's career or make money, so babies' chaperones are 99 per cent mums.

Thus professional chaperones are likely to be in charge of older children and teenagers. Such chaperones might indeed be regarded as professional stage mother substitutes. Diana continues:

> One chaperone may take charge of up to twelve children, but may not take on any other duties, which a stage manager or customer may find irritating ('No, I can't go and get you a coffee / help zip this dress'). Theatres regularly employ chaperones to take charge of their children's choruses; the local children's dance school may be called upon to provide the performers. Chaperoning a troupe of child performers in a theatre means knowing the running order of the show inside-out, ferrying the right child(ren) from dressing room to wings as required, usually in complete silence. You also need to know a whole wealth of silent finger-plays, card games, and tricks to stop the giggles—large chorus-size dressing rooms in council-run theatres are often situated right under the stage, so everyone has to be totally silent. On matinée days the chaperone(s) may also need to supervise the kids between shows, when it's best to escape to somewhere they can let off steam as well as be fed and watered and make their phone calls home —meanwhile making sure that their make-up and costumes don't get soiled.
>
> The chaperone may actually have more power than the director or producer, as the chaperone must ensure that the rules as to the length of time a child spends on set/on stage/rehearsing, etc., are strictly observed. This can literally mean shouting 'cut!' three quarters through a vital take as the child is due a ten-minute break. This takes serious guts and an air of authority.

* *Modelling and Acting for Kids* by Janice Hally; A & C Black, 2004, quoted here

For touring shows the chaperone must travel with the children and check out accommodation and so on, being on call twenty-four hours a day to deal with homesickness, etc. Sometimes the sheer volume of a project means setting up a whole new world for the child performers. The second Harry Potter film used over eight hundred children from schools all around the country, with one chaperone per twelve children, three travelling on each of the many coaches. My day was spent trying to pick out my allotted twelve teenagers and ferry them from coach to make up to costume to set to toilet to canteen to schoolroom and back, with interminable hours spent sitting with the crowd of chaperones at the edge of the set — we had to be kept off-camera and completely silent, checking off each child's chart of number of quarter-hours sent in each place, and silently voting as to who should be the one to tell the director that the kids were due a comfort break (at thousands of pounds cost to the budget).

The children, usually keen to perform and aware that bad behaviour would forfeit them the chance, rarely make the chaperone's job difficult. As long as you know several ways to entertain a crowd silently, how to deal with homesickness, broken friendships and teenage *Angst*, how to spot and discreetly remove a child needing a pee amid a crowd scene, and to organize a trip for thirteen to McDonalds in a town you don't know with a half-hour time frame, you have no problem. But you also need to deal with directors, stage door keepers, floor managers, adult performers, and parents. You need a real air of authority, and an inside knowledge of the industry certainly helps. You also need to accept that the job, particularly on a long-running stage or film production, may involve many incredibly tedious hours.'

— But such gallant professional stage-mother-substitutes have made a deliberate career choice to function in this way, and had appropriate training. Those of us who simply find ourselves in midlife in the position of natural-born stage mothers, willy-nilly, unconsulted, untrained, unqualified for the role, may feel mere astonishment at what has befallen us.

13 In Another Part of the Theatre

Diana then progressed to work in theatre management in London. Contact with the general public in this aspect proved fascinating. The first London production on which she worked was Willy Russell's *Blood Brothers*. Two ladies bought tickets for a matinée, and returned the day after the performance, commenting that it 'was not much about twins' as they had expected. They had in fact attended the wrong theatre, being shown to the corresponding seat numbers on their tickets there, and watched, uncomplaining, *Sherlock Holmes*.

Diana became Assistant Manager at Watford Palace Theatre while Stephen Keeling was staying with us; and motherhood, room-letting and the stage became closely integrated. While *Cinderella* was being prepared for Christmas production there, the Musical Director was taken ill, and Diana found the Stage Manager asking despairingly, 'Where can I find a rehearsal pianist by lunchtime?' Diana was able to

47

assure her, 'I've got one at home—shall I phone him?' Stephen became rehearsal pianist and deputy Musical Director for the entire run of the show (with Cinderella played by Morag Brownlie, who had sung the part of the narrator in *Piper* at East Herts College). As theatre lodgings, 'Carillon' proved a good career boost.

It was becoming a rare thing for me to have to pay for a seat in a theatre, with the pair of them, son and daughter, one behind the footlights and the other front of house. More often I would pass along a line of theatre staff, beaming and telling me how honoured they were to meet Miss Bell's mother, down to the one by the auditorium who would search my bag to make sure I was not in fact intending to blow the place up, daughter and all.

Theatre staff must remain at their duties long after the departure of the audience – and, indeed, the performers. Working in the West End, Diana finished work most nights around eleven, and travelled home alone from Piccadilly underground station—much cause for maternal concern. However, her only two encounters with crime were both on arrival at the railway station in genteel Harpenden, where her car was parked for the final stage of her journey home.

When I attended professional society meetings in London, finishing in the late evening, I would call at the theatre to escort her to King's Cross, then have to wait until she had finished work. Usually I was shown into the manager's box, right by the stage, to watch while I waited. I thus saw the last half-hour of *The Phantom of the Opera* many times, always seeing the face of the actor who advances downstage right suddenly register that the manager's box was now occupied.

Diana's place of work led to other dangers, too: terrorist bombs were frequent in the West End of London. For a while she would ring me quite often to report, 'There's been another bomb near the theatre, but I'm all right'. Then she told me quite specifically that she would make no more of these reassurance post-explosion calls: the day might come when she could not get through to me, and I would fear the worst, so in future, hearing of West End bombs, I was to assume all was well with her unless positively learning otherwise.

Her most terrifying experience during this period was when the London area around the theatre where she was in sole charge for the afternoon was sealed off because of a bomb scare, twenty minutes before the curtain was due to rise on a matinée performance. Some of the cast, staff and audience were already in the theatre; others were stopped on their way. No one could now enter or leave the building. Diana sent everyone in the theatre to the underground shelter of the stalls, herself remaining on watch in the foyer. Through the glass doors she could see a mounted policeman across the road. Suddenly, he grabbed and listened to his radio, then turned; looked directly at the theatre; dismounted and ran across to it. Heart thumping, she opened the door for him – and with exquisite relief heard him ask, 'Please may I use your toilet?'

14 From Hatfield to Vienna by Voice

Early in 1990 Aidan was faced with a major career choice. He auditioned for a Continental tour of the hippy musical from the '60s, *Hair*, and was offered a three-months contract to sing in this. At the same time, he was up for presenter of a children's series on Manchester television, and for another profitable commercial, and was offered an audition for *The Phantom of the Opera*. Moreover, Stephen Keeling, attending the Sondheim Musical Workshop in Oxford, maintained that, if Aidan would submit the score of *Piper*, he too would be offered a place on this. A choice had to be made, and Aidan, eager to travel abroad, settled for the tour, to the dismay of family and friends.

After playing in *Joseph and the Amazing Technicolour Dreamcoat, A Funny Thing Happened on the Way to the Forum, The Adventures of Huckleberry Finn, James and the Giant Peach* and *The Ideal Gnome Expedition*, Aidan was delighted to be in a musical with a short title.

He left England to join the tour showing an unwonted lack of confidence; he sat at Gatwick airport filling out an application form for projectionist work at the Hatfield soon-to-be-nine-screen cinema, in case his initial contract for the *Hair* tour was not renewed. A photograph was needed, so he went to the passport photo booth, which failed. A mechanic was called, repaired the equipment, and told Aidan he would have to take his pictures again. 'It's just like making a commercial,' Aidan observed: '"we'll have to do another take, Mr Bell"'.

Hair was a cult on the Continent, where a tour started in 1987 and had been running continuously ever since—sometimes with two companies touring simultaneously. It played in English, with American and English cast, changed frequently—it's a gruelling routine. Audiences were mostly German-speaking, but the musical, with its strong rock beat and well known hit songs ('Aquarius', 'Let the Sun Shine in', 'Hair') was not difficult to follow, and indeed audiences become thoroughly involved in it.

The musical epitomizes the '60s hippy teaching on war, theology, authority and sex—a social rebellion. The first act ends with the lead, Claude, singing 'Where do I go?' about the choice he must make between being drafted to fight in Vietnam, or dropping out to join the hippies' way of peace and concord, burning his draft card. The hippy tribe surround him, singing, then cover themselves with a huge sheet, emerging naked for the final cry, 'Freedom!'. The nude tableau, illustrating the vulnerability and unity of humankind, lasts thirty seconds, dimly lit. Remove that scene, and you have an hour and fifty-nine minutes of a fast-moving, exuberant musical, with large cast and many songs. Each cast member has several costumes: as hippy in daily life and at the Buddhist ceremony, as crooners, soldiers, figures in the hallucination scenes and the flash-back family scenes; 'Margaret' and her 'husband' emerging from the audience. Nevertheless, it is the nude scene alone that is recalled by anyone speaking of *Hair*, whether or not they have seen it. Friends hearing that Aidan was going into *Hair* all made one of two comments: 'Isn't that the nude show?'

49

or, 'Well, he won't have to worry about costume, then, will he!'

Performances were literally one-night stands, playing to a usually screaming, youthful, wildly enthusiastic audience that insistently demanded a succession of encores. Among this mob there sometimes sat one proudly smiling British matron, probably the oldest person present.

The show captivated me by including passages of Shakespeare set to music by Galt MacDermot. Claude's song, 'What a piece of work is man', is a soliloquy of Hamlet's; his death is preceded by a reference to 'star-crossed lovers', followed by three lines of Romeo's address to Juliet's apparently dead body, beginning, 'Eyes, look your last', and many repetitions of Horatio's greeting of Hamlet's death, 'The rest is silence', leading in to the final chorus, 'Let the Sun Shine in'.

Aidan, like all the cast in the tour, played several small parts. Perhaps the smallest was John Wilkes Booth, who does no more in the script than rise to his feet in the hallucination roll-call and answer 'Here, Sir'. Constant repetition grew wearisome; Aidan expanded and embroidered the role in many ways, wilder and wilder: once playing Booth as the Swedish chef from the Muppets, bringing on cooking ingredients and a frying pan – which in fact caught fire, on stage. On another occasion he dressed a life-size dummy in his costume and threw it from the tower down onto the stage, where it lay inert, apparently hurt, to the consternation of the audience. While their attention was distracted to the other side of the stage, he reached under the scenery and dragged the dummy back, quickly donned the costume again himself, and reported smartly to declare, 'Here, Sir', to the amazement of all.

Singing 'Old Fashioned Melody' in *Hair*, 1990

My trips to see Aidan's shows were becoming more exotic. Whenever the tour route showed more than two days at an interesting place near an airport, he would let us know; by fax to his father's research establishment, until the Director made objection to these unaccustomed exotic lists of theatres emerging amongst the scientific correspondence. Aidan's career, indeed, accorded as ill with his father's in science research as with my own in publishing. At home once, he phoned Colin at work, to be told by his secretary that Colin was in a colloquium. Not a familiar term in theatre circles: Aidan misheard this as 'in the cloakroom', and said he would ring back in five minutes. 'I don't think he'll be out by then,' said Jane. 'All right—I'll ring again in ten minutes'. 'I think it will take longer than that.' Aidan wondered what on earth his father was up to in the cloakroom, and why his secretary should know about it.

Colin and I flew out several times to Swiss towns to see Aidan and *Hair*. Our holidays thus became short, several, exotic, and culturally schizophrenic, touring churches and museums while the cast were busy, then often joining the highly hippy busload to travel to the theatre. The company were 'bus'n'truck'ing—travelling on the company bus, while scenery, costumes, sound and lighting equipment were sent some eight hours ahead, overnight, on a truck – as described in the lyric David Zippel wrote for Barbara Cook, 'The Ingenue':

'The parts you play quite often may require you to ham a lot
And you're inclined to wind up in a bus'n'truck of Camelot'.

Each day began with breakfast in a new hotel ('If it's Tuesday this must be Belgium'), then back onto the bus, where each of the troupe had their 'house'—a seat (double for the luckiest) with their luggage under it, pictures and notices pasted on their section of the window, where they rested, chatted or worked during the drive to the next venue—from two to eight hours' travelling each day. Aidan's 'house' also contained his typewriter, four-track recorder and synthesizer to enable him to carry on composing.

On arrival at each new town, the *Hair* company would disembark, settle in, and make for an often hasty pre-show meal, while the stage crew, who had travelled in advance with the truck, erected the scaffold set in the new venue, and the musicians set up the five-piece band. All types of continental venues were played: theatres, city halls, arts complexes, sports arenas, open-air—even the occasional church hall. Arriving at one such, when I was there, the horrified band members looked vainly for space for their instruments. 'Don't panic', said Noel Stevens, Musical Director of the production. 'When I want panic, I'll cue it: I'll go, one, two, three, panic.' Aidan reassured him, 'You needn't bother to play tonight—the vicar's wife can surely accompany us on the piano'.

Life on the bus could get very bitchy. The company members were in claustrophobically close contact, and their cultural horizons did not seem widened by their immense geographical spread. Few learned the languages of the countries they played in; they rarely explored their new environments. Aidan wearied of the fraught atmosphere, hired a van and drove himself and passengers from the band from venue to venue, sleeping in the van, self-catering or grazing in cafés. A girl from the cast

51

joined them in the van for a while, and with huge nostalgic enthusiasm Aidan enjoyed full fried English breakfasts in the British Army canteen where her English soldier boyfriend was stationed.

Other members of the company occasionally succumbed to the strain and flounced away. The understudy network was tight, each member understudying another with, in turn, a potential stand-in of their own. The understudy to the lead, Claude, vanished in a huff one night. A replacement from England was urgently sent for, and out came Paul, plucked from the chorus of *Evita*. Company management was somewhat flawed; Paul had been quite inadequately briefed, and supposed only that he was to play in the tribe (chorus) of *Hair* in Germany for two months. It was a shock for him to learn from his new colleagues that he was in fact on tour; that the show included a nude scene; and that he was himself understudying the lead. Should ill befall the Claude-player that day, indeed, Paul would have to play the part that night—despite not having been provided in advance with a script. Moreover, the cast were paid by the performance; until Paul had mastered the whole show, which has the entire cast on stage through most of it, and appeared on the boards, he would receive no money. He sat by me in the audience through that night's show on the day of his arrival, aghast to see all he would so soon have to do.

The English of the *Hair* management was uncertain. I was present when a manager made a rare visit to see the show, and, wishing to give the cast his outsider's verdict, began, 'I am an outstanding person . . .'. Gravely the company was told once that the police wished to search the bus for drugs, and were sending on a *duck* to sniff them out. Aidan wondered whether it quacked and laid an egg to signify success.

The company was indeed regarded with deep suspicion by drug authorities, with so much simulated drug-taking on stage in the course of the show. Returning to England by ferry from Holland after months on tour, Aidan caught the full brunt of this suspicion. He appeared as a template of the drug addict: long hair, bohemian dress, touring in a hippy musical, and coming from Holland where drugs are legal, so abundantly available. As he had in his car two dozen bottles of wine for his father's birthday, he went through the 'Something to Declare' lane at Sheerness Customs. The officers looked him over and stripped the car. They X-rayed the spare tyre, shone lights down the keyholes, removed panels, searched all cases, bags and boxes, scrutinized his videos. It took an hour, after which they had found nothing untoward. They then reassembled the car and allowed the wine through with no duty charged.

Hair was the first Western production to play in East Berlin after the demolition of the wall—Aidan brought home his own stones from it.

Diana, off for a skiing weekend with Andrew, lost a day to *Hair*. The show was to play next in Switzerland, but first the company had two days off, and Aidan had driven to Düsseldorf to stay with Conny. *En route* from the ferry port to the Austrian slopes, Diana and Andrew too stayed there overnight. After helping load their luggage into their car next day and waving them off, Aidan realized he had left his filofax, including his passport, in their car boot, and sped two hours up the motorway after them, but failed to catch them up. I received a frantic phone call: where was Diana going to stay? He must have his passport back next day to cross to Switzerland for the *Hair* performance. I had no address or phone number for her short holiday, and made

52

many phone calls trying to trace her, even driving ten miles to ask the neighbours who would be feeding her cats, and whose surname I did not know. (Directory enquiries would not divulge their phone number on being told merely, 'Hugh and Rosemary of . . .' with full postal address.)

Unpacking, though, at the far end of Austria, Diana discovered the passport and phoned Aidan, to be told that she and Andrew must drive several hours back to the border to despatch the passport through customs by the equivalent of Red Star to Düsseldorf. They obligingly did so; but it was a Sunday, and no train was leaving for Germany that day. They lost 50% of their skiing time to this enterprise. Diana now feels a sense of dread whenever she unpacks on holiday. Aidan missed the show and the relevant pay, entering Switzerland 24 hours late.

Freudiana, a musical by the British pop group, The Alan Parsons Project, based on the work of psychoanalyst Sigmund Freud, had opened at Vienna's Theater an der Wien in December 1990. Aidan auditioned for it and was taken on to join the show at its re-cast point, six months into its run. He left *Hair*, having toured with it for thirteen months.

After so long with the show, Aidan felt his departure should be marked. His last performance on the tour was in Zurich; he secretly hired a 14-strong brass band and rehearsed them in his solo song, 'My Conviction'. When his encore was demanded on the last night he signalled to the band waiting in the foyer, and they marched, playing, into the auditorium, up the aisle and onto the stage. The cast were as amazed as the audience by this invasion of the stage; the band members themselves (not English-speakers) never quite understood what they were doing or why, but enthusiastically remained for the rest of the show and the subsequent farewell-Aidan party.

A few days later *Hair* played in Frankfurt, near where Aidan was then staying. He drove to the theatre and entered backstage, secretly again, made up as a ghost, and wafted unannounced across the stage during the hallucination scene, to the stupefaction of the cast, who were unsure whether they were really seeing him or hallucinating indeed. On leaving the stage he disappeared from the building and drove away, becoming part of *Hair*'s legend.

Touring in *Hair* had given Aidan a fantastic experience, which he relished to the full. He played in ten countries, with so many miles driven, such scenery, the different cultures and cuisines sampled—few other careers could have offered him all this as a perk. Certainly his parents could not. Just as Ian's cult computer game had raised him way out of his parents' income bracket, so Aidan's first overseas musical tour gave him a taste of travel we could never have provided for him.

15 Margaret Rules!

When he first went into *Hair* Aidan played the part of Hubert, the husband of 'Margaret Mead', an effusive, middle-aged lady who surges out of the audience to question the men in the cast about their dress and style, in the parodied manner of the anthropologist Margaret Mead investigating the tribes of Samoa and New Guinea. She stays on stage to sing a falsetto number reaching to high C sharp, 'My Conviction', about male display – 'That is the way things are in most species': a passage by the real Margaret Mead, in fact, set to music. The revelation that the singer is a man should come as a shock at the end of the scene.

At first Aidan was also Margaret's understudy. When the current Margaret went the way of so many disgruntled cast members, making a sudden departure, Aidan took over the role, making full use of the high, pure falsetto voice he could produce, in strong contrast to his powerful, belting rock.

The *Hair* wardrobe mistress took Aidan to the shops as chaperone and adviser to purchase a suitable costume; he inherited the previous Margaret's wig; and the girls in the cast taught him to make up appropriately. He learned that wearing two pairs of tights obviates the need to shave male legs to play a woman, and that in a skirt you walk with smaller steps and never sit on stage with your legs apart.

Aidan's long arms extended way beyond the sleeves of Margaret's blouse, and to camouflage these he wanted a supply of bangles and rings. Switzerland, land of superbly crafted jewellery, did not trade in cheap costume stuff, and had but few second-hand shops. Aidan phoned to ask me to buy cheap, junky rings for him. On a day in London for editorial meetings, I went into souvenir shops to buy some, and was surprised to find that they sold plenty of trashy ear-rings, brooches and pendants, but no rings. At last I tried jewellers; but asking these for rings costing less than £2 was greeted with no more respect for the customer than asking chemists for false-moustache glue had been.

Having to play the part of a middle-aged, middle-class lady, Aidan imitated the one he knew best—myself. With wig, glasses, skirt and blouse, my genes and mannerisms, he appeared extraordinarily like me, so that I would sit in the audience and apparently watch myself on stage, in an out-of-body experience. The company were told, before my visits, that they were about to meet the original Margaret; and I was always addressed as Margaret by the cast of *Hair*. In one photograph of Aidan as Margaret with Kirk Duncan he looked so like me that I would show it to friends and ask, 'who's that?'. They would usually reply – 'Well, that's you, but I don't know who the man is'.

I fantasized about taking over the role; if Aidan should miss his cue (on arrival at each theatre, he had to work out how to make his way from the dressing room to a seat in the audience after changing into Margaret's costume), surely I could call out his opening lines, 'Young man! young man! May I ask you a question?' and keep the dialogue going till he arrived. I would threaten to beat him to the line, which had to interrupt the stage dialogue at that point, and take over—Noel, the Musical Director,

Leon Snevets and Margaret Elisabeth Assarowa — aka Noel Stevens and Aidan, 1991

being much alarmed to overhear this. In fact Aidan would begin his Margaret-protests, 'Really! This is dreadful! Why are they dressed like this?', seated in the audience, in advance of his final cue, which often led to hostile shushing from those seated nearby.

Aidan's performance as Margaret proved very popular, with encores demanded almost nightly. He devised a series of these, singing 'My Conviction' as Eartha Kitt; in German (translated and rehearsed by Conny), with thigh-slapping; yodelling; once, when they played in a circus-tent, on stilts, and another time, arranging a flying harness in which he rose far above the stage and hovered as he sang.

Never one to perform just one job at a time, Aidan developed a cabaret act based on Margaret, with himself as 'Margaret Elisabeth Assarowa, the defective Russian Princess' who sang 'Songs from the Shows' Julie-Andrews style —'I could have danced all night'; 'I feel pretty' (Margaret declaring, 'I have sometimes been told that I am not the most attractive of women. While this might daunt a lesser lady, I simply reply that it's how you feel that counts, and *I feel pretty*'), and Noel as accompanist. They played all the night-club bookings they could get, after the curtain came down on *Hair*.

The act grew into a splendid characterization with impressive vocal range. Margaret became a separate personality of whom we spoke in the third person; I would suggest to Aidan that a new song would be good 'for Margaret to do'. Aidan was pleased to tell us eventually that Margaret, mettlesome lady —'a thin relative of Dame Edna', one reviewer called her — was greeted with more applause on her entrance in his cabaret performances than he was *in propria persona*.

After leaving *Hair* Aidan no longer had Noel available as Margaret's accompanist (Noel remained as M.D on the *Hair* tour for five years). He asked his friend Kirk Duncan, veteran keyboard player of many pop bands, to drive Aidan's car out to Vienna, for him to keep there; they would try to establish a cabaret act together. Kirk agreed, but discovered only on setting out on his journey that his passport was three years out of date. He pointed this out to the passport controller at Dover, who said that he didn't mind but could not answer for the controls at the other borders. Aidan met him at Ostende and they drove together through Belgium, Luxembourg, Germany and into Austria with not one person actually looking at their passports.

After lingering for three weeks in Vienna they had had only one cabaret booking and Kirk had to return to England, the poorer for the venture. He went to the British Consulate in Vienna to apply for a temporary passport, but it would have taken too long to arrive; he and Aidan gave up, drove to Düsseldorf and stayed at Conny's overnight. They were greatly frustrated to receive there a phone call asking them to perform cabaret in Vienna. Kirk's refusal of the booking was unprintable. The next day he travelled by train through Germany and Belgium again; his passport was checked at Ostende without being recognized as out of date. It was not examined at Dover, as it had been checked at Ostende; and Kirk arrived safely home in Southend. That was in 1991 ...

Aidan was asked to sing as Margaret at a wedding reception in Vienna. He gave them Puccini's 'Nessun dorma' from *Turandot*, 'in which I play the part of Dot' he explained, introducing it. He borrowed from a Viennese theatre the gown Evita had worn there for the balcony scene, and sewed into the skirt 200 Christmas-tree lights. These were switched on, as well as four fountain-fireworks behind him, as he reached his final top D. He thus upstaged the bride, who was also wearing off-the-shoulder billowing white, less technologically enhanced.

Margaret's wardrobe grew, and came to cause some embarrassment when Aidan left his second flat in Vienna. Prospective tenants being shown round, knowing Aidan lived there alone, would stare into the wardrobe, boasting full-length gowns and purple feather boa, without liking to ask ...

16 Back at the Ranch

During his years working on the Continent Aidan made occasional short visits home – when he would particularly appreciate seeing the same room on waking each morning, and hearing his own language spoken in shops and streets. One particularly brief visit – or swoop – was made to attend the London auditions for the Palladium production of *Joseph and the Amazing Technicolour Dreamcoat*. Aidan determined to try for this, although it would mean his driving through the night to a Swiss airport after the evening's performance of *Hair*, then proceeding on arrival straight from Heathrow to the audition theatre, having not seen a bed since curtain up the night

56

before. After the audition he would have to return to Heathrow to catch the evening plane back to Switzerland and *Hair* – spending less than a day in England.

He arrived in a snow-bound, frozen England, where most transport was immobilized. I had agreed to meet him in London, and hardly liked to suggest that while he could make the trip thither from Zurich, it was too difficult for me to travel the twenty miles from Hatfield. We met for lunch in Piccadilly, Aidan bearing duty-free wine and a huge Swiss gateau for his parents, which I had strict instructions to keep THIS WAY UP. He also had a package of publicity materials for the musical *Elite*, to be delivered (by me, of course), to an address in Belsize Park. A former colleague in *Hair* lived there: her flatmate was shortly to leave for America, and had agreed to promote *Elite* there, if he got the materials that day.

Aidan, after so many hours of sleepless travel and performance, was too tired to perform properly at the audition, and even absent-mindedly made his thanks and farewells there in German. He was not cast on this occasion. After the audition he had one more hour in town before he must start the journey back to Heathrow. We walked to Dress Circle, 'The Showbiz shop' in Covent Garden, where he updated his collection of CDs of musicals, then left the country. I set wearily off on my snow-bound, cake-and-wine-laden trip to Belsize Park to introduce myself to yet another singer with my catch-phrase, 'I am the mother of Aidan Bell'.

On another brief return home Aidan's career again impinged on my own as a freelance editor. His old room would not accommodate all his accumulated luggage, which remained strewn round the living room. Stephen Keeling came to stay, sleeping on a mattress in Aidan's room, which was moved out to the living room in the morning to allow them room to dress. Then, just after the boys had left for a day in London, a printer rang me, saying, 'we have some queries over the last disc you sent us—could I call round in twenty minutes to discuss them?' As this printer had been selected for the journal in question partly because of the short and easy journey between my premises and theirs, I had to agree, devising a critical path analysis for action.

The previous year I had spent some months working fulltime in a large firm's publications department. There, I would have rung reception to arrange for the caller to be admitted and directed to my office; perhaps asked for coffee to be brought in for us both; and assembled all the relevant papers from the files while I waited.

This time, working at home, mentally juggling priorities, I first removed all the luggage and bedding from the living room in which I would discuss the disc with the printer. This is not the polish-the-furniture, arrange-the-flowers hospitality syndrome, but the at-all-costs-avoid-the-zany-amateur-freelance-image imperative. By the time the printer arrived, the room was tidy and free from alien objects, but I was breathless, far from calmly poring over my papers.

On these visits home Aidan was anxious to see as many London shows as possible, and I seized the opportunity to go too, making theatre visits of an unaccustomed frequency. The day after we saw *Kiss of the Spider Woman* we went to the musical film, *Beauty and the Beast* in the afternoon, and *Assassins* at the Donmar Warehouse in the evening—an extraordinary amount of death, disaster and battle in musicals encountered within twenty-four hours.

Our appreciation of shows did not meld well. Often, as we left, Aidan would ask

57

eagerly, 'Did you like . . .' naming some particular piece of over-production which I had missed, having closed my eyes at that point. I object greatly, and with sore eyes, to the modern tendency to accompany important passages of stage action with laser flashes and strobe lighting. Warning notices are placed for those subject to epilepsy, but I suspect that many people find the assaults on the retina stressful. The audience might be found to be sitting in rows with eyes tight shut, crossly waiting for the lighting designer's self-indulgence to be over, occasionally peeping timorously to see if the visual ordeal is over yet, if any theatre management cared to investigate. I ask only for skilled performances, subtle, witty or moving script, melodious music and graceful or exuberant dance, from my seat in the audience: disbelief should be suspended by those alone. I know just where I am, and will not be convinced by scenery or lighting that it is sunrise, sunset, the Sahara at noon or Black Alley at night. All that I ask from the lighting is to be able to see the performers clearly, having neither to peer into the gloom nor defensively lower the eyelids. But it seems that because stupendous lighting effects are possible, therefore they must always be used. Aidan, child of his generation, loves them – but they don't suit mama.

Perhaps it is in order to hoard the current for these terrible glaring flashes that insufficient lighting is provided for the audience to read—whether over-priced programmes or matter they have brought with them—while waiting for the show to start. Why must we sit then in semi-darkness? Is it to key up our sense of anticipation—or to ensure that *anything* that happens afterwards to relieve our boredom will be warmly welcomed?

17 Casting, Casting

On tour Aidan had formed an alliance with a Viennese producer, and together they agreed to mount an Eastern European tour of a musical. Aidan had a few weeks in England between leaving the tour of *Hair* and starting rehearsals for *Freudiana* in Vienna, in the summer of 1991. He devoted this time to setting up the touring production – to be Pink Hippo's third, following *Piper* and *The Devil and Mr Stone*.

Their first choice for a musical to tour was *Jesus Christ Superstar* (with Aidan's record of devotion, it had to be), but after much effort they failed to obtain the rights. They then began negotiations to put on *The Rocky Horror Show*. This took much time and several meetings, introducing Aidan to the world of the business lunch. His Viennese partner, Christian, flying over for one, was stranded with us overnight when Pavarotti sang in Hyde Park—the effect on London transport was catastrophic, and Christian reached Heathrow too late for his flight home. By the time the *Rocky Horror Show* rights were secured, Aidan had only three weeks left in England.

He placed an advertisement in *The Stage* calling for CVs and photographs from applicants for the ten-strong cast. The English office was our bungalow, and Diana and I became honorary staff for the exercise, with a paid helper, Jon, a drama-student-to-be. It was fascinating; and showed me how close Aidan's career as producer was to my own as editor. Opening, categorizing and responding to the resulting mail, I came to see theatre production as a sort of editing in three dimensions, dealing with actions rather than words, people instead of papers. I also learned to regard some types of theatre agents with a very jaundiced editorial eye.

Like editors, producers select, groom and amalgamate the work of a group of contributors, striving to keep relations cordial and standards correct, to achieve eventually a composite new whole. Like many authors, some aspirants to the stage seem to pay little heed to stipulations about submissions, or to copy dates.

Our advertised deadline for receipt of applications was a Saturday. On that day, and again on the Monday, Tuesday, and Wednesday of the following week, our massive theatre mail came in a special van; for some time thereafter we continued to receive daily bundles. There were also deliveries by hand, faxes, and pleading phone calls.

Opening it all was heart-breaking, knowing that only three girls and seven boys, plus two understudy/swings, could be selected. We received in all about 800 applications. The majority were clearly talented and eager, with serious, professional presentations; good glossy 10" x 8" pictures in stiff-backed envelopes. Still, 790 or so would have to be rejected regardless. Some 60-70% of the applications were for the three girls' parts, the odds against them thus even more heavily weighted.

A sense of desperation seeped through, distressingly. They knew the statistics of applying for stage jobs, needed work, wanted this tour, and strove to stand out and be noticed, favoured upon. They enclosed poems; pleas; several copies of the same CV; cassettes; outrageous photographs; letraset notices, 'PLEASE PLEASE PLEASE PLEASE AUDITION ME', 'Look no further – you have found your Frank'N'Furter'. One stuck a teabag to a witty letter. But you stop smiling and gasping after opening the first hundred or so.

We stapled each photo on top of its accompanying CV, with covering letter at the back, and sorted first into four piles: loonies / boys / girls / multiples.

The loonies were the obvious to-be-discarded (the editorial junk papers, to me): sprawling handwritten accounts of paper rounds or YTS work in warehouses folded small and crammed into tiny envelopes, offcuts from photo-booth strips spilling out unattached. Others were more intelligent but still sloppy or unsuitable, and badly presented. Sending a 3" x 5" s.a.e. for the return of a 5" x 8" photograph indicates a lack of serious reflection. So does 'Film and tv work: negligible', conscientiously included in a CV: hardly stressing one's strongest features.

Boys / girls was an essential first division, but seemed not a possible one for many of the agents' submissions, where several clients' CVs and photos were often sent together in one envelope with a single covering letter. The worst agent sent the most clients, without even a list, in a flimsy, tearing envelope, understamped. We paid the excess postage, glared at the dozen photographs, and tried not to blame the actors for the shortcomings of their agent. No problem, that; we came to pity them thoroughly.

Multiple applications at first went in the fourth pile, but there were too many. We had to sort them into boys / girls, separating them thus from their covering letters, which were assembled in another pile, while boys and girls were subdivided into fair / good / outstanding. There were also small special categories— Aidan's friends and

59

colleagues, who would need personal replies; unsolicited applications for posts such as wardrobe mistress, translator, etc.; dwarfs (we had not advertised for these, but some who had seen the film version of *RHS* applied anyway); and body-builders. One of these, a singing/dancing one, moreover, was essential to play the part of Rocky, but known to be a rare commodity.

The schedule was tight. We went through CVs on Sunday, Aidan took them to the Director on Monday and they drew up the lists to call for auditions. On Monday evening and all Tuesday three of us rang the chosen ones, compiling a schedule for 35 ten-minute slots each on the Wednesday and Thursday. The selected CVs were gradually sorted again into booked for audition / waiting reply / can't reach / can't attend audition / reserves / etc.

Ringing the actors who'd applied direct to us was a joy. Their addresses and phone numbers were attached to their photos, easy to find, and their delight was apparent down the phone. It was a help to us to be able to make the calls in the evening—but you can't ring agents' offices then, and we had no home numbers for the actors whose applications had been made through agents. Agents' clients who hadn't been contacted by Tuesday evening had to be left till office hours on Wednesday —and not early ones.

Early on the Wednesday Aidan left for the auditions in London while I opened that morning's hundred or so late applications. Eight slots that afternoon were still empty. I had a pile of CVs to ring in specified order —the last chance for eight lucky applicants from our eager 800.

After 9 am I started phoning, working down the prescribed pile. I was also hunting body-builders, ringing strange men to inquire about their muscular physique if I thought their photos, late arrivals unseen by my son, looked hunky.

Again, calls to the actors' homes elicited joy and rapid agreement to audition that afternoon; agents' offices provoked only answerphones, and I couldn't leave any of the eight places to be tied up awaiting replies that might not fill them in time. The first agent who answered his phone got *two* of his actors in, the second one promoted from the bottom of the pile—a reward for actually picking up his ringing phone. Other agents did far worse by their trusting clients.

One agent had moved some time before and was still sending his clients' CVs out with his former, now obsolete telephone number—the new number was only on his one-copy-between-them-all letter. Luckily for his clients, his successor on the previous line answered the phone and gave me the new number, which I rang, to be told by an answerphone, 'If it's urgent we'll ring you back after six o'clock'—this about 9.30 am. I devised a mantra, '*It's not the actor's fault if the agent messes up his chances and loses the producer's goodwill*'. One agent had put no address, no phone number, nor even the agency name, on the CVs—only on the once-accompanying, overall letter. It took quite a bit of rummaging to identify the letter and find the number, as well as determination not to let the actor suffer for the folly of the agent. It was some months after London telephone numbers were prefaced with 071 or 081 instead of a uniform 01. Several London agents' numbers were still prefaced 01—no indication whether to insert 7 or 8. One was printed without even 01. I dialled the number I saw; got the voice telling me to try 071 or 081; guessed wrong; got through the third time, invoking the mantra.

The most obscure agent seemed to be floundering. 'He'll have to bring a rock song', Diana said yet again into the phone. 'A love song?' 'No, a rock song.' 'How do you spell that?' 'R, O, C, K.' 'Anything else?' 'He'll need to move.' 'Move house?' Another puzzled me by asking whether his client, auditioning for the role of Columbia, should bring her shoes. Yes, I said, thinking, what an extraordinary question. Aidan explained that he meant, would she have to perform Columbia's tap dance?

Actors compete to get agents, regarding them as essential career props and paying them a good percentage of their earnings. We found that many agents acted as barriers rather than bridges between producer and potential cast. It would have been easiest for us to abandon the applicants whose agents made access to them onerous, with such a superfluity to choose from. After that exercise, casting a musical from advertisement to audition, I consider that many actors would do better to promote themselves, individually, efficiently, and directly, with carefully copyedited CVs. Perhaps they need editors more than agents.

The film director François Truffaut would concur. According to Julian Barnes's collection of essays, *Something to Declare,*'When an agent tried to push an actress on to him, he replied, "If I may judge from your letter, from the way it is typed and laid out, and the condition in which it arrived, complete with documents, I should say that Mademoiselle X might best be offered the role of an illiterate slut".'

The second day of the auditions in London was, for me, the most chaotic. Aidan, Diana, and Jon were all there: I was alone with the Pink Hippo telephone, still besieged by would-be *Rocky* players. There were road-workings outside the hall near Piccadilly Circus that had been booked for the auditions; on the second day the drilling proved so noisy that the auditions had to be relocated. No way to let the hopeful arrivals know where to go instead but to pin up a notice on the door of the venue first notified, and give details of the new location to me to pass on to anyone who phoned.

Then Aidan phoned too. He had realized that his only chance to sleep from the next morning, Thursday, until Friday night, would be on the ferry crossing he had booked from Sheerness to Vlissingen. Would I please book a sleeping cabin on it for him? Highly necessary. I rang the travel agents in Hatfield town centre. As the crossing would be from ten in the morning to five in the afternoon, the travel agent found this requirement for a cabin surprising, and wondered if I might be confusing a.m. and p.m. I convinced him of the need, but was told I would have to bring Aidan's ticket in to be stamped, could not book a cabin over the phone. This would mean my leaving the Pink Hippo phone untended. I considered the best course of action: decided that keyed-up actors arriving for audition, finding an empty hall, ringing their only line for guidance and getting an answerphone would succumb to total hysteria; an engaged signal would at least reassure them that human life was there, and they would try again. I took the phone off the hook, drove as fast as possible to town, parked, booked, returned, and re-established telephone contact.

Diana also found the auditions stressful. The director asked all prospective Frank'N'Furters whose free-choice singing he had liked, 'show us how frightening you can be'. My young daughter, sitting beside him, made a splendid target for the actors' terrorizing powers, all of which they directed at her.

61

After the first two days of auditions, recalls were held on the third, followed by a final casting session over dinner in London between Aidan, his co-producer and the director. That same evening, Aidan had to drive back to Hatfield; load his car with all he could get in that he would need to furnish his flat in Vienna and to continue to compose and record music there; sleep if there were any time, then drive through the night to Sheerness to catch the ferry, cross to Vlissingen, and drive on to Conny's flat in Düsseldorf for a much-needed rest *en route*. On arrival in Vienna he would go straight into rehearsal for *Freudiana*. Kindly, as I thought, I offered to drive him to Sheerness myself and come home by train, so he could sleep in the car. I was told, though, that there was no room in the crowded car for a mere mother—saucepans and Margaret's wig-stand were more highly valued occupants of the front passenger seat.

Back at the ranch, we sent out huge bundles of 'thanks but no thanks' letters to most of the 800 who had replied to the *Stage* ad. And I had a sad week or two, constantly answering the phone to anxious inquirers about their chances, and telling them, sorry, it was all over; breaking a heart every twenty minutes, I felt.

Aidan flew back to England briefly for the first meeting of the *Rocky* cast, held in the Director's house on the coast near Colchester. Diana, Jon and I drove there. Aidan was still anxious to conceal the fact that Pink Hippo's address was not an office block but a bungalow, and the phone most likely to be answered by family members; so in introducing us to the cast he avoided using the name 'Bell'. Having introduced Jon by his full name, 'I'm sure you've all spoken to Diana on the phone', he said as he indicated her, and all smiled and nodded. He looked at me, and murmured, 'And that's Hazel from the office'. As an editor accustomed to attend conferences where full courtesies are observed, I felt a distinct drop in status.

Jon, the son of a Hatfield Vicar, was appointed assistant stage manager for the tour. Before it started, one afternoon when he and Diana were both at their day jobs, an urgent question came up about costumes for the show. I tried to ring Jon at home, and was taken aback to find myself discussing the fishnet tights to be worn by the *Rocky* cast with the Vicar.

18 Horror in Hungary

In Vienna Aidan was earning his most steady money yet, with regular hours, always in the same place, in *Freudiana*. The Theater an der Wien company management impressed him deeply; a dressing-room with dresser to each three actors; apartments provided for cast members, and insurance coverage (so long as they remained in Vienna). But this regular life, singing seven parts for six performances a week, was not enough. He had to moonlight, producing *The Rocky Horror Show* at the same time, commuting to Budapest, three hours' drive away, and out of contractual bounds.

Rehearsals and the first week of the production were to be in Budapest. Setting up arrangements in advance, Aidan established several friendly contacts there. He wanted his parents to benefit from this to the extent of an exotic holiday, and we enjoyed a splendid one, flying first to Budapest, travelling on by train to Vienna for a week with Aidan, then back by train to Budapest for a week there before flying home. Jon, meanwhile, came into 'Carillon' daily to deal with the Pink Hippo post, telephone calls and faxes, and feed our cats.

Aidan arranged for us to be given a guided tour by one of his Hungarian contacts. We came to regret this: tales of Magyar inefficiency proved far from mythical. On the day of the tour we had to hang around our hotel waiting for the guide until 4.30 pm, missing our planned day's shopping. The taxi she hired for us ran out of petrol on the motorway out of town, leaving us stranded in the heat at the roadside while the driver trudged off with petrol can. When we finally arrived at the village we were to see, its shops were closing.

The class system prevailed in Budapest. I deplored the timorous humility and subservient smile of the violinist who hovered over the tables in the hotel dining room, playing his instrument at (I choose the preposition advisedly) the diners, table by table. Listeners were to tuck currency notes under the strings of his violin, as it might be down the dress of a gypsy bride, or the jockstrap of a Chippendale.

Our holiday was during the last two weeks before the assembled Pink Hippo touring company was to depart for eastern Europe. We knew we were flying back from Budapest on the day they were all to fly out, and we would indeed reach Heathrow shortly before their departure—probably on the same plane. We duly touched down, passed through customs, made the two-hour underground and British Rail journey back to Hatfield, and arrived home weary, longing for tea and a session with the backlog of post for freelance work. The answerphone light was winking. It was the *Rocky Horror Show* narrator: 'I've missed the plane. I'm standing by the information desk at Heathrow. Will someone please ring me back and tell me what to do?'

He must have been standing there ever since we left the airport.

Jon was on the plane with the rest of the cast, and we knew that Aidan and all the Vienna office staff were at a press conference for the show. No one to consult about the plane-misser except Diana, then Deputy Manager at a West End theatre. I phoned there and, asking to speak to Miss Bell, was told, 'She's seeing the house in. Can you ring again in twenty minutes?'. Introducing a pitiful quaver to my voice, I said, 'Yes, thank you. Would you tell her that her mother would be very glad to hear from her as soon as it's convenient?' 'I'll get her at once', I was assured. Diana, on being told to ring her mother, knowing of our complicated travel arrangements, asked, 'In Vienna, Budapest or England?' 'Do you know, I never thought to ask', said the secretary.

Diana's own week's 'holiday' in Budapest on the strength of this production was even more bedevilled by catastrophe. Her expectations on arrival were not rosy, after her first flight to see Aidan on the Continent. On that occasion he had promised to meet her at Vienna airport, then phoned me in Hatfield on the day to say he had an extra rehearsal, she wasn't answering her phone, would I tell her of new arrangements. I explained that the reason she wasn't answering her phone was that she was already *en route* for Vienna, so I couldn't phone her either (these were pre-mobile phone days). Aidan said never mind, he'd leave a message for her at the airport.

On arrival at night in the strange country on that occasion, Diana found no brother

63

to meet her, and waited some considerable time before realizing that the incomprehensible German sounds coming over the loudspeakers included something that sounded like 'Diana Bell'. She went to the information desk, and was told to take a taxi from the airport to the Theater an der Wien in the city centre. She did this – which took a large proportion of the money she had saved for her holiday.

Now, when Diana was flying out for a working holiday on *Rocky*, Pink Hippo production funds were running low. She was not met at the airport (rehearsals/late productions/meetings usually prevented Aidan meeting any plane he had agreed to), and because of Aidan's also locking himself out of his car, found herself wandering alone in Budapest at 3 a.m., brotherless, hotelless, and lost. Instead of her promised hotel room, she got a couch in the apartment of Katalin, the Hungarian Public Relations Officer. She worked as production manager for the last, fraught week of *Rocky* rehearsals, salariless also. Shortly after her arrival in Budapest, Aidan decided he must leave for PR duties in Vienna. At last, much longed for by his sister, he returned, on a week's leave from *Freudiana*.

Aidan had phoned us often and despairingly in the final week of preparation; then we heard nothing on the first night of *Rocky*, nor next day until he rang late in the afternoon. 'Darling —how did it go?' I eagerly asked. 'What?—Oh, the show—well, it was all right—well, not really—Mum, I'm all right now and I'm back in Katalin's apartment, but I'd better tell you . . .'

Aidan, reunited at last with his sister, after a series of production disasters, had displayed all the symptoms of a heart attack that morning, and been taken by ambulance to Budapest hospital, between Diana and Katalin, each holding one of his hands and weeping. Diana tried to convey to the Hungarian attendants, 'My other brother once suffered a pneumothorax with similar symptoms'; Katalin, as interpreter, could not cope with that sentence. Diana knew that Aidan's Theater an der Wien

Diana as a crew member for *The Rocky Horror Show;* Budapest, 1991

64

insurance covered him only in Vienna, and was dreading phoning her parents either to tell us of the death of our younger son, or to ask for a cheque to cover open heart surgery. However, after many tests on Aidan, Katalin passed on the tidings that he was suffering from a leaking pulmonary artery (*sic*, that's what she said, or what he said she said), caused by stress; and should drive himself back to Vienna to consult his own doctor there.

Fortunately my lack of medical knowledge protected me from recognizing how grave a condition such a leak would have been, and I merely lamented in general over the international phone line and asked whether there was anything a mother in Hertfordshire might do to assist her ailing son in Hungary. Well, yes, explained Aidan, there was. All his problems were due to stress, the doctors agreed, so the best way to help would be to relieve his stress. The *Rocky* production lacked any more funding, but the actor playing the extraterrestrial transvestite Frank'N'Furter, who was too short for the part and had to wear shoes that would give him extra height as well as alternative gender, needed another pair for a costume change. These shoes were very expensive, could be obtained only from a specialist theatre shop in London, and were causing Aidan more stress than anything else. So I could best help his recovery by ordering another pair of these shoes, please. But unfortunately the bill for the previous pair had not been paid, so it would be necessary first to pay that bill.

I did this, making one of my many phone calls that began, 'You don't know me, but I am the mother of Aidan Bell, and I believe . . .'. I paid the incredible three-figure cost of the shoes, looking on it as payment in lieu of Aidan's medical bill. (At the sight of his British passport and distressed sister, the hospital in fact made no charge for the diagnosis.) I was in London the following day, at a conference on the publication of scientific papers, and left it in the lunch hour to meet the shoeman. I did so all the more eagerly having asked a Professor of Physiology at the conference, 'Is it serious if you have a leaking pulmonary artery?' He told me gravely, 'Oh yes—in fact you would die'.

Whether Aidan's condition had been misdiagnosed, or his diagnosis mistranslated from the Hungarian, we never learned.

As instructed by his medical advisers, Aidan drove his car back from Budapest to Vienna, his sister, little invigorated by her holiday, beside him. He arrived at the theatre for the *Freudiana* performance late, and reversed into another car in parking. A *Polizist* loomed up, and clearly would not settle for a hasty, 'Can't stop—due in makeup'. Diana was despatched to the theatre to explain that Aidan was back in Vienna but delayed, would appear in that evening's performance, and the understudy was not to take over his parts and his pay. Diana spoke very little German; but having managed, '*Mein Bruder ist Aidan Bell*', was met by understanding nods on all sides.

65

19 The Spice of Life

With the touring company for *Rocky* composed, and Aidan back in Vienna, I found an unexpected patch of a few days' freedom from my freelance work. Such patches are rare, and usually unforeseeable. Colin and I wanted to seize the opportunity to spend a few days touring the Lake District. The Pink Hippo phone could not be left untended at this stage of production, though, and we stayed home instead through the hot summer spell. Gratefully, Aidan asked Diana, as Pink Hippo Secretary, to arrange for a huge bouquet of flowers to be delivered to me. When she subsequently passed me the Company accounts to fax through to the Vienna office, I explained, mother to daughter, that it is not customary to give such a gift, then display the bill to the recipient.

A bonus remained from the passing of the bungalow casting of *Rocky*. The fax machine that had been installed to keep Aidan in contact with the Vienna office remained in mine, in Hatfield. The fax was registered as Pink Hippo's, though, and that name appeared on outgoing message sheets, unless I pressed a button Aidan programmed for me. The name appeared, too, as the recipient on the records of those sending messages to me. I found it embarrassing, after berating printers for the lateness of their proofs and insisting that they be faxed to me immediately 'at this number', to have the ensuing fax followed by a ringing phone and a printer convulsed by hilarity asking, 'Can you give us your fax number again—it's all gone somewhere called Pink Hippo!'. 'I am Pink Hippo' is a reply that lacks dignity.

Later I worked for a few days in a London journal production office. I had to obtain permission to leave its number on my own answerphone for Pink Hippo callers, and for such unaccustomed calls to be accepted in the learned society department.

After Pink Hippo had ceased to operate, and Aidan and Diana had both moved away from Hatfield, our Pink Hippo telephone line was given an outgoing-only-message. Aidan's voice explained with some emphasis that we had no costumes for hire, that Pink Hippo operations were suspended, and gave Diana's new home telephone number for personal messages. It was not uncommon for desperate seekers of fancy dress to ring the Pink Hippo number, misled by the local directory; then ring Diana's home, where her answerphone gave the number of whichever West End theatre she was currently working at; and, thirdly, ring that theatre to ask to hire a costume. The stage door keepers learnt to pass such unaccustomed requests to Miss Bell.

I had long since become accustomed to the hazards of working professionally, freelance, at home, with children. When I first gave up teaching to stay at home as a mother of young children, I took up indexing – the compilation of back-of-the-book indexes. My first published index was to a biography of Elizabeth Garrett Anderson, the first English woman doctor; others that I compiled in those stay-at-home, child-rearing years included the ones to Sacheverell Sitwell's *Monks, Nuns and Monasteries*, the memoirs of Konrad Adenauer and Georges Bidault, and *Erotic Art of the East* (there was some concern over that one as to whether the Post Office would transmit the illustrations).

The worst moments were when employers telephoned while a baby was actually crying on my lap, or visiting children joining mine in an uproarious game which I could not inaudibly subdue: how consoling once on a business call to hear another child crying at the other end of the phone! Ah, another freelance working mother ... Mine learned young that they were an indexer's children: Not Fiddling With Mummy's Cards was a major taboo, especially after Diana was found about to abstract all the pink ones from a set ready for typing – yes, for indexers those were the days of 5" x 3" cards in shoeboxes, not-yet-electric typewriters, and carbon paper. My children had their own "indexes", old cards of mine in boxes, which they removed, pencilled and replaced as to the manner-born — which indeed they were. At two years old, Aidan made a great impression at the infant clinic, looking at a tray of record cards and lisping, 'Is that the lady's index?'

Years later, schoolgirl Diana, having answered the phone in my absence to find the Library Association seeking to place an advertisement for a thesaurus in a journal I edited, left me a note that showed how helpful she had tried to be, asking what she thought I would need to know Her note explained, 'It is a kind of book'.

But freelance working life as the mother of an actor was a whole new can of worms — though not without its appeal. The day would never lack variety, with plentiful interruption. A typical morning was spent trying to write a report of a conference on copyright law. The phone rang constantly: people wanting a Groucho Marx moustache or Mickey Mouse costume from Pink Hippo; a former colleague of Aidan's, now on tour in *The Magic Roundabout*, looking for a six-foot tall actor to take over urgently as Dylan; an offer for a journal of an article on indexing French verbs in reverse alphabetical order; and Aidan, telling me he had had all the publicity material for *Piper* translated into German by a student currently acting as his PA, was about to fax it through, and would I please type it right away into my computer to produce leaflets and posters by desktop publishing?

Working solitude was often relieved by Aidan's old friends and colleagues calling to keep in touch or, too late, to say goodbye before he left again for the Continent. I enjoyed many a long chat with them, in lieu of my son. Reading the newspapers at home took on an extra dimension, selecting items to send to Aidan in exile. The chosen pieces would be reviews and notices of musicals; anything about Cameron Mackintosh, Tim Rice or Andrew Lloyd Webber.

In another frantic phone call Aidan wailed that he had been told he had been misadvised months before about his visa requirements, was in fact an unwittingly illegal immigrant in Austria, must have a visa or he could not work in Vienna (let alone rent his flat and drive his car). Could I find out what he had to do?

I rang the Home Office, then the Austrian Embassy, and explained his case. By the next morning he had worked out that the Embassy was the place to apply, and rang them direct himself, giving the same case history. 'Are you the son of Hazel Bell?' he was asked, from all those borders away. This was a rare instance of mother making an impression on son.

Much variety was lent to my own writing, usually articles for learned journals, by being called on to provide the occasional lyric: an entry for a Eurovision song contest, to fit a tune of Aidan's; or an attempt to express the grief of Hamelin parents in lyric form for *Piper*. Then Aidan applied to broadcast on Blue Danube (the main English-speaking radio channel in Austria, luckily located in Vienna), as a presenter, or to discuss and review musicals. He was asked to provide an outline for six half-hour scripts for a series, 'The Modern Musical': a commission passed on to his mother, more of a word-monger, who found it a bracing change from academic publishing. We would fax pages of scripts back and forth, Aidan providing the facts and value judgments, I the phraseology and punctuation. I made this unpaid commission the excuse to buy several cassettes of musicals, playing them in my office as 'my research', and attending a series of Sunday afternoon 'Lost Musicals' presentations at the Barbican Theatre, which I greatly enjoyed.

We produced together six half-hour scripts for 'The Modern Musical'. The first,'Plays with Music', examined the respective importance of text and music in musicals, and their integration; 'Hey, Mr Producer!' the process of mounting a stage musical; 'I Am What I Am', criss-cross sexuality in the musical; 'From Stage to Screen and Back Again', compared musicals in theatre and film versions; 'All the World's a Stage' – the seven ages of man as depicted in musicals; and finally 'The Musical in Vienna'demonstrated the development of the form there. Each broadcast of course was illustrated by playing appropriate numbers, and each had a distinguished guest interviewee.

I learned that the scripts had been accepted when an Interflora van drew up outside my window to deliver a huge bouquet and card reading, 'Congratulations on your first script for Viennese Radio'. (This has never happened when my articles have been accepted for publication in journals.)

I can report that hearing one's child perform something that one has written oneself brings a double sense of creativity, most rewarding.

For the broadcasts, again, the family name could be used only for Aidan. My credit as script-writer was under my maiden name, while Diana, interviewed as theatre manager about the habits of audiences at musicals, was 'Diana Rose'—from her second name, Rosamond.

Usually my research is historical or bibliographical. After phone calls from Vienna, though, where Aidan was preparing printed programmes for his shows, I would have to ring the County Music Library to ask for the composers of such works as 'Why do men say I've got such a wonderful pair?'; 'Mr and Mrs Hoofer at home—that's H, O, O, F, E, R'; or 'Sing'—such an uninformative title that to identify it I had to carol into the phone, 'Sing, sing a song, sing out loud, sing out strong . . .'.

However, during this period, monitoring Aidan's crisis-ridden life on the Continent, despite all distractions, I managed to continue to compile indexes and to write articles. Colin meanwhile received many calls about Aidan's English car in Vienna, diagnosing its ills long-distance, and obtaining and sending out spare parts unobtainable in Austria.

Crisis phone calls from one's young are extra distressing when there are seas and hundreds of miles between you, whether they concern leaking heart's blood, laryngitis on the day of a major performance, failure to find a flat, stolen passports, missing visas, unemployment, poverty, or dangerous, undiagnosable car faults.

20 Soul-searching to Music

I flew to Vienna again to see Aidan in *Freudiana*, enjoying staying in the beautiful city, fascinating sights to be discovered on every exploration. In the evenings we ate in the beer gardens, warm on summer nights, lit by strings of hanging lights. I was particularly taken by their *Hühner-schnitzel*: chicken breasts, beaten flat, breadcrumbed and fried, spreading over entire plates, seeming half a yard across. 'Chickens here must be proper Clara Clucks', I told Aidan, remembering Disney's vast-busted hen soprano.

Freudiana proved to be another musical involving scholarship – Freudian theories of psychoanalysis. The characters include the protagonists of some of Sigmund Freud's most famous cases – the Wolfman, the Ratman, the Judge, Dora, Anna-O and Little Hans – as well as Maitre Charcot, the French hypnotist, singing 'Let Yourself Go'. In the English version the overture is titled 'The Nirvana Principle'; the song, 'I am a Mirror' presents the function of the psychoanalyst; 'Funny You Should Say That', the interpretation of dreams; 'Upper Me' the Ego and the Id; 'You're on Your Own' the mother/son relationship; 'No One Can Love You Better Than Me' the Oedipus complex; and Dora sings 'Beyond the Pleasure Principle'.

Like *Hair*, this show also involved nudity, with a naked Adam and naked Eve appearing on stage for a prolonged scene – but without the provoking outcry caused by the briefer, dimmer nude scene in *Hair*.

The book and libretto used in Vienna were in German; the complex plot proved incomprehensible even to those who knew the language, I was assured by the cast. It was hard for the leading players, who portrayed The Universal Mother and Father in a series of manifestations: in a circus, a nightclub, a highly symbolic tunnel, as well as domestically. Their costumes and behaviour were so different in each scene that many of the audience did not realize the same actors were playing throughout, and their versatility went unappreciated. Aidan, playing a boy scout (the tallest in the movement, surely), half a circus horse, a hospital orderly, a nightclub punter, an underground passenger, an elderly disciple of Freud, and a mysterious monklike figure, had no such problem sustaining unity of role.

A producer-friend of Aidan's, Frank, came out to see *Freudiana*. He fell for it totally—music, movement, set, everything. Over dinner afterwards he was eagery planning to buy the production and bring it to London. Aidan pointed out that London had only one stage large enough for the huge, complex set of *Freudiana,* which consisted much of huge hydraulic mirrors. 'That's all right', said Frank, 'we'll have to buy out Cameron. He can move *Miss Saigon*.' No, it didn't happen ... that remains the only occasion when I have seen a show escorted by a would-be purchaser.

While appearing in *Freudiana*, Aidan did not have sufficient time off to come back to England for Christmas. He spent that one, 1991, at Conny's family home in Oberreute,in West Germany. It was more than ten years since Conny and Aidan had first met, so fittingly, at the *Superstar* stage door; he wrote a song to her about that, which included his proposal of marriage. As Conny's parents had no piano he took a

69

keyboard specially there with him, and having set it up in their living room, to Conny's bewilderment, he played and sang his proposal to her – and was of course accepted, on cue. The couple phoned us that Christmas day to tell us of their engagement.

Now we were to have another family member in a stage career – I would be a stage-mother-in-law, indeed. Conny was working in a theatre in Düsseldorf, and would have to give up this job if she joined Aidan in Vienna, on spec to find work in the theatre there. They would marry when Aidan had achieved a reasonable income. It was to be a long engagement, and distantly conducted. Both of them working in theatres, each had only Sunday free, not a whole weekend, and the distance between Düsseldorf and Vienna was too great for them to get together and back in a single day.

Oberreute is a charming village in the mountainous region of the Allgäu. Each summer the cattle are taken up the mountains to graze, then back to the village when winter comes, attended by a procession. Aidan and Conny were there one year when the cattle were due to return, and determined to get up early in the morning to witness it. Alas, they stayed up too late the night before, and were awakened by the sound of many cowbells ringing. They had literally slept until the cows came home.

21 Viennese Ventures

Eager as ever to promote *Piper*, Aidan managed to mount a *Sponsorenpräsentation*, a demonstration performance of five songs, in Conny's German version, at the Akzent Theater in Vienna. Professional performers agreed to appear free in this; most of them from *Freudiana* (shortly to close) or *Phantom*. The Hamelin rats rehearsed their dance late at night, after the *Freudiana* curtain came down. A few days before the show the girl who was to play the Mayor's daughter lost her voice to laryngitis, and a substitute was sought. Aidan was told of a *Freudiana* dresser who intended a singing career. He auditioned her in the interval, having had his costume and makeup change into a elderly professor speeded up so that, in beard and top-hat, he had time to coach her and hear her in the daughter's song; she got the part.

Attempts to get a Viennese Boys' Choir member to sing the part of the lame child of Hamelin failed, but a good, sturdy young singer from a choir of high repute arrived. It seemed churlish to complain that this boy, who sang well and did all he was told, looked too well-nourished for the pathos the part required.

My part was to design and lay out publicity materials and programme, in German, of which I knew little, working letter by letter. Colin and I flew out again for the show, and I called up my hoarded graciousness to exert upon the potential sponsors, though in a foreign language this came harder.

A designer friend from *Freudiana* created a large polystyrene wedge of 'Emmental cheese' with rats burrowing into or emerging from the holes as a prop centre-piece for the after-show buffet. This splendid artefact subsequently dominated Aidan's living-room – a conversation piece indeed.

Invitations to the show – as in Welwyn Garden City five years before, no charge;

refreshments provided, as it was intended to attract sponsors. – were for 4.30 p.m. The cast rehearsed all day, stopping to retire to dressing rooms and prepare in earnest for the performance at about 4 o'clock. Those involved in reception, including gracious me, took up our positions in the foyer. At 4.25, with no audience arrived, I was ready to weep for all the generous,wasted effort. Then, at 4.30, it was like the scene in *Zulu* when the hordes swarm over the hill-crests. Viennese theatre-goers, a polite ten minutes late, taking it as a social rather than a theatre occasion, arrived *en masse* from all directions.

A coachload of Hungarian journalists and TV crew was to attend and video the performance, but arrived an hour late. They loved the show, and were keen to produce a Hungarian version. A new title would have to be found, though: *Piper* in Hungarian has a second, obscene meaning.

Just as in Welwyn Garden City, the show was wildly applauded; no subsequent production was achieved; and large sums of money were lost. Pounds, schillings, deutschmarks – *Piper* can lose them all.

Freudiana closed in 1992, eight months after Aidan had joined the cast. By then he was well established in Vienna, with a flat, two cats, several useful professional contacts, and a rising reputation. He decided to stay there, despite never having mastered the language. This lack seemed extraordinary; but the touring *Hair* company had been all English-speaking and the show played in English; German Conny spoke fluent English; many musicals in Vienna are played in English (as one who most appreciates the witty, subtle lyrics of such masters of the form as Tim Rice, I would hold them untranslatable), and the theatre circles in which Aidan moved all spoke it. He could order meals and do his shopping in German, and sing his lines in *Freudiana*, but little more.

A series of stage-struck students proved eager to act as PAs for Aidan for musical productions, including as interpreters and translators, as well sometimes as lodgers and cat-feeders.

Full of enthusiasm for his Viennese radio series, 'The Modern Musical', Aidan flew back to England for a few days and interviewed Tim Rice and Cameron Mackintosh for the programmes. His pay, though, did not cover his fare. This is typical Aidan economics.

I found it ironic that Aidan was interviewing Tim Rice. He had been a devoted follower of his through all the stages of his career. In his earliest years he revered Rice as the lyricist of *Jesus Christ Superstar*. Aidan had sent him fan letters. Then he seemed extraordinarily lucky in attending the same musicals performances as Rice, and would seize the opportunity to speak to him. Before one of our annual visits to *Joseph and the Dreamcoat* at Westminster Theatre in the late '70s, indeed, Aidan seemed to expect Rice in the auditorium as part of any proper theatre outing, and would find it falling short of expectation if this were lacking. He had used the tenuous connection of their communal school teacher to meet Rice backstage after *Evita* with Gary Bond. Aged 16, he managed to be photographed with Rice and Lloyd Webber at the closing party of *Jesus Christ Superstar*. Later he sent the score of *Piper* to Rice, who wrote a friendly letter saying that he could not pass an opinion on it as he could not read music. Now Aidan was discussing with Rice the problems of translation of

71

lyrics, of revisions of productions, of writing for film rather than stage, for cartoon rather than real characters, for broadcasting. His high opinion of Rice remained, from an adult perspective.

Money was sorely needed after the financial drain of the *Sponsorenpräsentation,* and Aidan went back into the still-ongoing tour of *Hair* for another two months. (Returning to *Hair,* and becoming a counter-tenor in church music, were two strongly contrasting reserve contingency careers Aidan contemplated should all else fail.) This time he finished in Odense, Denmark. Colin and I flew out for a Danish holiday, and to see his final performance in *Hair*. Aidan allowed me this time to realize my fantasy of preempting his appearance as Margaret and call out at the right point in the show, from my seat in the audience, 'Young man! Young man! May I ask you a question?'. When the cast uneasily invited what they could see to be the wrong person to come up on stage, Aidan rose by my side, with, 'Don't worry, dear, *I'll* go. My sister wants to know ...'. So I can now add to my CV, *brief appearance in rock musical in Denmark.*

Odense is the birthplace of Hans Andersen. The cobbled street of his childhood home is carefully preserved, offering a fairy-tale-visiting walk (it was used as the setting for early scenes in the film, *Hans Christian Andersen,* with Danny Kaye in the title role); there are statues of figures from the stories in the Andersen Gardens – strange to see a concrete representation of a paper boat in real water!

Before flying home from Copenhagen Airport, we took a train to Elsinore to see the very castle of Claudius and Hamlet, thus completing a strangely diverse cultural trio in a single week – *Hair,* Hans Andersen and *Hamlet*. Elsinore manifested less appreciation of its literary associations than Odense. I had planned to send holiday postcards showing the brooding prince, but there was not a trace of the Englishman Shakespeare to be found anywhere, save one comic monk figurine holding a skull in the touristic shop, which otherwise had only the usual twee or comic postcards and irrelevant fancy goods. Shakespeare and Hamlet were loftily ignored throughout the town of Elsinore – except for the Ophelia Restaurant, where we could have ordered Shakespeare barbecued ribs.

As Thespian parents, we were doing our own cultural tours.

22 Rocky II

At last, though, further proper theatre work with proper pay was achieved. Aidan, having himself produced the version of *The Rocky Horror Sho*w that played in Budapest and toured Austria the previous year, attended the auditions for a 1992 production in Amstetten, to be directed by Alexander Goebel, who had recently sung the role of the Phantom in Vienna, and choreographed by Kim Duddy, who was responsible for the dancing in *Freudiana* (and at whose wedding Aidan had sung 'Nessun dorma'). The production was to be in German, with only the songs in English.

Aidan was cast in the role of the butler/alien, Riff Raff. We received another of our many shock phone calls from him: he was going to sacrifice his hair for his art.

No light decision for him; he had cherished his thick locks, styled in many ways through the years by 'my hairdresser' in Potters Bar, eight miles from home. It had been at different times short and wavy; shoulder-length; bleached; permed; during the *Hair* tour, plaited into dreadlocks – always carefully considered, deliberately presented. Now, for *The Rocky Horror Show*, after much discussion with colleagues, and assurances that the hair would grow again afterwards, he felt it incumbent on him to go bald, as Richard O'Brien (author of the show as well as its original Riff Raff), Terence Kelly (in the Pink Hippo production), and many others, had before in the role.

I thought sadly of the similar sacrifices (for money) of Marty South in Thomas Hardy's *The Woodlanders* and of Jo March in *Little Women*. Poor Jo was greeted by her thoughtless sisters on her return from the scissoring with, 'But Jo, it was your one beauty!'

Aidan and the new *RHS* producers seized the opportunity for publicity from the shearing. The deed was done surrounded by film crew, with champagne served, and shown on Viennese television. We have the video in our family memorabilia.

We sighed, but accepted the prospect of a skinhead son for two months—till the planned end of the run of this *RHS* production. Aidan, though, once he had become smooth-scalped, found he actually liked it. With his large eyes and strong features, wide-eared, he did not appear, as Marty South is told by her insensitive lover, 'like an apple upon a gate-post'. He came to like the distinctive head-style so much that he kept it for some years, using a cartoon of himself emphasizing bald dome, huge eyes and ears, as his logo, printed on all his publicity material and even ghosted life-size on his headed letter-paper. He acquired a collection of headgear; in the summer, extended the rubbing of sun-cream over his scalp; in winter, discovered how cold a hairless head can be, and donned a thick, black, Russian fur hat, bought on the *Hair*

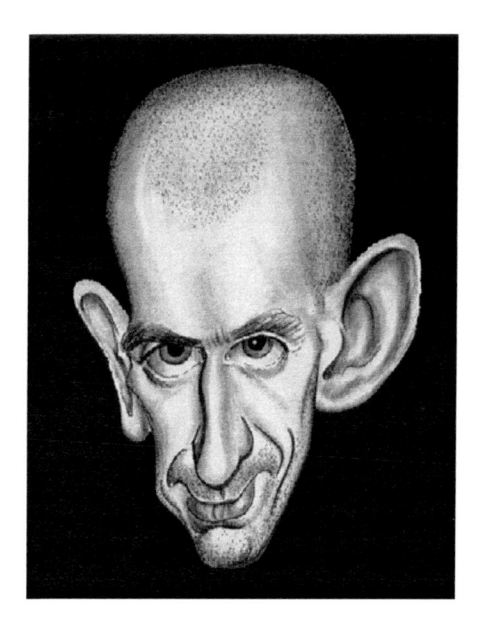

tour in Berlin.

Back in England, cold scalp covered by fur hat, he visited Frank (unsuccessful in his envisaged purchase of *Freudiana*), who had a new baby. (I heard him phoning Frank later, saying, 'Your daughter is adorable —if you don't want her any more, send her DHL to Vienna, and I'll look after her'.) A health visitor arrived while Aidan was there, and hearing that the baby was shortly to be taken on holiday with her parents, asked, 'And who will look after your beautiful cat?, apparently basking on a soft chair. With some embarrassment, Frank explained, 'That isn't a cat—it's Aidan's hat'.

Baldness was no handicap in returning to *Hair*, in which of course Aidan wore a wig as Margaret, and he was given a new additional role to play, that of an Indian guru. This character, too, he has frequently reused in cabaret since, and wrote a comedy song for him, 'Summer Singalong'.

Some months after his remarkable recovery from a leaking pulmonary artery Aidan had occasion to visit his Viennese doctor once more. As he entered the surgery he prepared to recount the tale of his last visit, thinking the doctor would not recall one patient after so long, particularly with the disguise of a shaven head. But he was greeted with, 'Ah, Mr Bell. Have you had any further problems with your chest?'

Aidan expressed surprise at being recognized after becoming bald, and was told, 'I watched your hair coming off on the television. I thought, "I hope you will wear a warm hat or your head will catch cold".'

Colin and I had to fly out to see Aidan as Riff Raff, of course. I told colleagues I was leaving for some days in Vienna. 'How lovely—why are you going?' they would ask. My reply, 'to see *The Rocky Horror Show*' seemed inappropriate.

Aidan's transformation from butler to alien at the end of the show was effected by a spectacular costume and make-up (necessitating the shaven head), of which he was anxious that we should receive the full impact in performance, with no spoiling preview. The huge photograph of him in that costume was removed from his

Riff Raff the butrler, 1992

Riff Raff the extraterrestrial, 1992

living-room wall and hidden before our visit, and the programme he gave us to take to the show had paper strips stuck over all photographs that included Aidan. He drove us to Amstetten, an hour out of Vienna, where the show was playing, and left us to look round the town while he prepared for the performance. We had to promise to avert our eyes from the posters plastered everywhere, lest they should include photographs of him.

Amstetten was not a typical venue for the well-established *RHS*. The audience there was soberly dressed and behaved—except for a handful of *RHS* habitués who arrived wearing the more customary crimson and black, displaying gaudy underwear, and called out some of the traditional raucous responses during the show. These include 'Kinky!', 'Damn it, Janet!', 'Lick those lips!', 'Don't touch the hair!', and plenty of very much stronger language. The actor playing the narrator was not accustomed to this, and did not like it. At a point half-way through the show when he had the stage to himself, he sternly told the audience (in German – Colin and I could not think what was happening) that their behaviour was disgraceful, and unless they watched the performance in proper silence he would call the police. Rarely are *Rocky* performances so strictly disciplined.

After the show, Colin and I reported to the stage door as arranged, and asked the stage door keeper to let Aidan know his parents were there. Over the Tannoy system, repeated with a German accent, Aidan thought he heard, 'Will Aidan come to the stage door where his pants are waiting'.

While Aidan was still playing in Amstetten, when Colin and I were back at home, one evening our phone rang. I answered it, heard a piano being played, then Aidan's voice, apparently exercising. I listened, bewildered as to why he'd phoned me at trans-Continental rates to treat me to this private performance, but assumed he had some reason for doing it, and, long though this near-cacophony continued, was loth to ring off, thinking my son would be hurt by my dismissal. Eventually the music stopped, there was silence, and I ventured a hesitant, 'Aidan?' into the phone. I heard his astonished voice asking: 'Mum! What are you doing there?'

Aidan had put his mobile phone down on the piano to do his warm-up before the show, and inadvertently pressed my ID button on it. I had thus heard a very expensive private recital; Aidan was relieved that he had not pressed instead the ID button for his agent or a producer.

23 Continental Crossings

Freudiana at the Theater an der Wien had played on Sundays, with Wednesdays off, while *Das Phantom der Oper* at the Raimund Theater played on Wednesdays, closed on Mondays. Thus Viennese hoarding lights were able to boast, 'No night without a musical'. When both shows closed, early in 1992, Vienna had an unaccustomed dearth of musicals. Enterprisingly, Aidan decided to seize the opportunity and fill the gap. Unable after all to mount a production of *Piper* following the *Sponsorpräsentation,* he circulated the players from the closed musicals and other shows whom he knew to be between jobs, suggesting that they should combine and utilize their talents in a compilation-show. He invited them to meet at his flat (offering them the wine remaining from the *Sponsorpräsentation).*

The idea was enthusiastically received, and a theatre that had been little used for years, the Applaus, was revived to house the show. For this first venture, the cast of seventeen were paid expenses only, with the prospect of sharing any profits. Each chose their own items to perform, solo or in conjunction. Alexander Goebel was director; Aidan, producer; Noel Stevens was Musical Director, assembling a six-piece band. The show was played in both German and English; Aidan sang the romantic ballad, 'Meadowlark', bald head concealed by a colourful cap.

The show's title, *Musical?—Oh My God . . .,* was the last line of the song Aidan wrote for its finale, reflecting his view of his parents' attitude to his career choice:

There is a story that when I was a kid
My father asked me one day
Did I know what I was going to do
When I finished school and went on my way?
That's when I told him what I wanted in life,
I asked if that was okay;
But my father sighed and he simply replied,
That it really all depends on the pay . . .
I said 'I want to be a singer in a musical show'
And he said, 'Musical?—Oh my God!'

The finale included a mosaic of snatches from various musicals played and mimed – tantalizing to identify as they segued swiftly into each other, slickly choreographed:

Little Shop of Horrors, Les Miserables, Evita, West Side Story, Jesus Christ Superstar, ... there was particularly rousing applause when, for the final quote, Goebel crossed the stage costumed as for his original role of Phantom in Vienna. The star cast in chorus looked like a Who's Who of Viennese musical theatre – Uwe Kröger, Pia Douwes, Kim Duddy, Aris Sas ... The audiences loved it.

I flew out to see it. Seeing Aidan's shows was becoming an expensive business. I had always intended to see all his performances, and thought driving to pantomimes and musicals in Bristol, Liverpool, Manchester, Glasgow and the Isle of Wight, and sitting through children's matinées about gnomes having holidays on traffic islands, and Stanley Baxter's thick and raunchy Glaswegian—following all the years of maternal audience-escort duty—had been sterling motherhood. Now I was almost commuting to Vienna—a costly habit. It also meant that Colin and I had no more foreign holidays elsewhere. We wanted to visit Greece, Spain and Venice, but if you know you are going three times in a year to Vienna, you don't feel justified in making a trip to Athens just for the foreign feel of it.

I would have to take out with me diverse items of luggage for Aidan: videos, home-made cakes, wigs for Margaret. One piece of black electrical equipment, wires trailing, I showed despairingly to Customs, hardly expecting to be believed when I told them 'My son uses this to write music'. And always, always, bottles of Biactol, sold by Boots for acne, unobtainable in Vienna, and plentifully used by Aidan to counteract all the greasepaint. I bought so much Biactol I felt like wearing sunglasses and high collar to sneak into Boots. 'Does he drink the stuff?' asked Diana.

Sitting in on a band rehearsal for *Musical? —Oh My God . . .*, I found it odd that the letters A, B, C, etc., were used to mark sections of the musical score, while also serving as notation for the keys. I suggested that Noel—M.D. again—should use Roman numerals instead to indicate sections. Most of the band professed not to know what these were, but Noel cued their next piece, 'One, two, three four—*veni, vidi, vici*'.

I went to the after-show party with ambivalent feelings. I was aware of being an outsider, not even speaking the language, a generation above those involved in the show, in a profession dowdy by comparison with Show Biz. Aidan had often found mixing me with his friends embarrassing, screaming at them to recall the presence of his mother at the third repetition of their favourite adjective. I would explain that I was liable to swoon at the eighth. On one occasion I felt like the little girls who intrude into a psychiatric lecture in Mel Brooks' film, *High Anxiety*, so that the discussion of sexual development is continued in baby-talk to spare their young ears. I reprimanded Aidan for recounting some mishap to colleagues with too much ribaldry, and he modified his account to, 'Oh dear, I made a really bad mistake'.

But I knew, too, the power of the producer. Aidan had as yet made no money himself from any of his enterprises, but it lay with him to bestow parts, promotion and pay upon aspiring actors. Many of them, being introduced to this insignificant Englishwoman, had straightened up and shaken my hand with renewed vigour on learning I was Aidan's mother. (Though the actress who gasped, 'His mother? But he's so talented!' was a little galling.) I recalled one phone call from an actor inthe Pink Hippo production of *Rocky,* some weeks after it was over, telling me that only

77

two of its cast had achieved theatre work since, and he had returned to teaching. When he asked after Aidan, and I mentioned that he was preparing a production of *Piper*, I could hear the stiffening of the ears, the twitching of the nostrils, the change of tone as he assured me that he had rung only to make friendly enquiries as to what we were all doing now, he'd had no idea there was any possibility of parts in prospect . . .

So, at the *Oh My God . . .* party, conservatively dressed English pedant as I was, I told myself firmly, '*I am the producer's mother*', and sailed in amongst the glitterati to launch into discussion of the relationship of the lyric to the musical form and its difference from opera with all comers.

The show was a huge success. After five nights at the Applaus it played again in Bratislava. It was recorded live by X-ART Studios Mobile, and released on CD; finally a live version of the CD was performed for two nights at the prestigious Vienna Konzerthaus, with the cast by now even receiving salaries.

I flew out again to see the performance in the Konzerthaus – a building more usually presenting Mozart concerts. There was much press attendance, with drinks and fraternization in the foyer afterwards, which I missed, dressed to the nines for the occasion as I was. Following Aidan to the foyer after the much-applauded show, I was asked, 'Vere are you going?' Turning, I saw the wardrobe mistress, Hilde, a German lady of my own age. 'I'm following Aidan', I told her; and heard, to my astonishment, 'Zat is not a good idea. I sink you should come viz me'.

Aidan was now out of earshot; surprised, I accompanied her as instructed, though I balked at being told to get into her car – 'Does Aidan know?'. 'Oh, yes, he has asked me to take you zere'. Some Aidan-organized surprise in store, I assumed. We drove for some time, parked, and walked through the public gardens where an impromptu after-show party was to be held. There, we sat in the cold night and waited for more than half an hour for other party-goers from the show. It later transpired that an English member of the cast, with what he claimed to be a peculiarly English sense of humour – I would repudiate it for my country – had pretended to have lost one of his contact lenses on the stage (he wore none), and had the entire cast crawling over the stage searching for it, kind-hearted, for a long, vain time, while Hilde and I shivered alone at the gardens.

Eventually, members of the *Oh My God ...* cast began to join us, reporting Aidan as running round the Konzerthaus proclaiming, 'I've lost my mother!' At last contact was made, Aidan joined us, and the sequence of events was sorted out. Hilde had told him she would not come to the party, as she would be on her own; he had said, 'Oh, no, you can go with my Mother'. Unfamiliar with English, she had interpreted this as, 'Take my Mother there', and ground into immediate, peremptory action.

Aidan still cherished the desire for a professional production of *Piper*. When the *Sponsorpräsentation* failed to find the necessary sponsors, he was told that part of the reason was that he was not sufficiently well known. The answer was obvious – achieve fame. To this end, Aidan decided to put on a one-man show, and did this at a small theatre, the Residenz, with the challenging title, *Who the Hell is Aidan Bell?*.

This was the first show Aidan appeared in that I missed (first time round). When I had promised myself to see them all, I did not anticipate his career overseas. He phoned to tell us of the coming one-man show just a week after I returned from my

A couple of song and dance men in *Who The Hell Is Aidan Bell?* 1993

second trip to Vienna in a year, when I had already booked the third (me that had been accustomed to French camp sites and the week at Clacton holiday camp). He sent us a video of the show, which had been made as a promotional tool for him, so we watched that in lieu of attendance. It seemed to show great bias: while it was fair enough to focus on Aidan as he sang, told stories, performed as Margaret and in his Indian guru role, I thought it hard, while his one guest artiste, Michael Seida, tap-danced, to focus on Aidan accompanying him on the bongos.

We were learning the sad truths of the finances of theatre production. There seem to be three types of earnings. For careers in regular employment, you receive regular pay, even in periods of sickness, holidays or idleness, with redundancy handouts, pensions and unemployment benefit available. Secondly, freelance workers (such as me) are paid only for the hours we actually work—nothing for sickness or holidays, or to sustain us between commissions. As for privately mounting a theatre production—any financial rewards are speculative only. The more you pour into a production, the harder you work, however great the resulting success in artistic and professional terms, the larger may be your financial loss—and with no welfare state fallback. Most of Aidan's enterprises fitted the classic line, 'The operation was a success, but unfortunately the patient died'. His productions brought him high acclaim, increasing local fame, glowing reviews couched in German obscure to his mother, fan mail, professional colleagues and contacts—but no commensurate financial reward—quite the reverse. My son, the honoured pauper.

24 Rocky III

To make my third visit to Vienna in 1993 I had to cancel a meeting of the Editorial Board of a learned journal. I hardly liked to explain that this was necessary so that I could attend the première of *The Rocky Horror Show* at the Raimund Theater in Vienna. The production from Amstetten, with Aidan as Riff Raff, was to play in this prestigious theatre, lately vacated by *Das Phantom der Oper,* for six weeks, to mark the 20th anniversary of Richard O'Brien's composition. This was a year of nostalgic revivals; in London, *Hair, Godspell, Grease* and *Carousel* were all being restaged. Vienna got *Rocky* redivivus.

I spent six days in Vienna for this proud occasion, and found the short visit combining opposite extremes of my complex life as editorial mother of an actor. One difficulty about the frequency of my visits to Vienna was the constant breaks in my freelance work. Nearly all my editorial and indexing work had become computer-dependent, so I could not often take work with me to continue on the journey and in Vienna (no laptops yet). On the day of my departure for this trip, I was pleased that a 46-page draft arrived of the revision of the British Standard guidelines for indexing. This I could take with me, and I read and annotated it all through the journey, on train and plane.

Dressed in my most glittering outfit, I went to the *Rocky* première the next evening, with Conny and Wilfried, Aidan's new PA. Most of the audience were dressed outrageously for the occasion in black and red featuring prominen, corsetry, with much cross-dressing and ghoulish make-up. Conny was dashing in a man's black suit with a kiss-curl; Wilfried, coy in red jacket with black tights and high heels. He minced flirtatiously through the crowds, except that each time he saw a camera – of which there were many – he hid behind us, gasping, 'My mother mustn't see me like this on television'. I admonished him, 'Tell your mother, if I can take it, she can take it'.

The party after the show was held in the disco of the Technische Museum (yes, it had a disco – don't they all?), packed, with central platform for further performance, and 'Frank'N'Burgers' served by McDonalds. Richard O'Brien himself attended the first night and the party. Highlights from the show were performed again, and Aidan was thrilled to find himself singing Riff Raff's hit song, 'The Time Warp', together with O'Brien. Aidan and Conny had spent a day choosing new clothes for him for the party; as he belted out, 'It's the pelvic thrust that really drives you insane – let's do the Time Warp again!', he was actually thinking, 'I'm so glad I went to C & A'.

Richard O'Brien, Alexander Goebel (former Riff Raff in Vienna as well as Phantom, and Director of this *RHS* production) and Aidan all alike had shaven heads, dating from their Riff Raff days, and the bald trio provided a splendid subject for photographs, at the centre of a throng of cameras – heaven for Aidan. For the second time that week, I peered at my son from the back of a crowd – this time, not one of autograph hunters but of photographers.

Theatre hours are strange; a main meal before an evening show would be both

Three Riff Raffs: Alexander Goebel, Aidan and Richard O'Brien, 1993

unwise and very early for the performers. Aidan always ate after the show, around midnight; then, usually, he and Conny would watch a video 'to relax' before going to bed around 3 a.m. (Although he quite often appeared on Viennese television, in extracts from performances or interviewed with an interpreter, Aidan rarely watched the television programmes, all in German.) I would go to bed when in Aidan's flat at about 12.30 a.m., after this unaccustomed late dinner. Next day, I would get up about 10 a.m., while all other occupants of the flat, video-regaled, would sleep till midday. I would have the problem of how to spend the morning in this strange flat, which I could not leave because of the logistical problem of the front door and the two cats. The living room was filled with sleeping musicians (I slept in Aidan's office).

I found two contrasting ways to occupy these hours. The flat was filthy; it was due for refurbishment by the landlord the following year, and until then no maintenance was being done. In these solitary morning hours I cleaned all the paintwork, walls, doors and windows that did not actually shelter sleepers; the transformation was so complete that it was positively pleasurable (though I felt ruefully aware of falling into the stereotypical housework-obsessed-mother role played by June Whitfield and Maureen Lipman). I also taught myself to use Aidan's Apple Mac computer, a type I had never worked on before. Once that was mastered, I typed a three-page commentary on the British Standard, and the basis of an article on how phonetics and the demands on the larynx of singing musical notes constrain the vowel sounds of singers, and therefore should constrain also the vocabulary choice of a lyricist for musicals – thus making lyrics more difficult to write than pure poetry. Aidan, once awake, was able to put me in touch with a Musical Director from whom I could commission such an article.

25 Impresario about Town

Two days after the *RHS* première at the Raimund, X-ART, the recording company that had made the CD of *Musical?—Oh My God* . . ., was opening new premises, a high-tech sound studio at Pinkafeld, an hour's drive out of Vienna. This was to be launched with open-air performances of items the studio had recorded, from 8 p.m. on. Aidan was to produce half an hour of excerpts from *Musical?—Oh My God* . . .; but this could not happen till around midnight as he and some other performers were also appearing in *RHS*. He arranged for three car-loads of performers and companions to be driven from Vienna to the studio; the first car was to make an early departure, as radio and TV crews would be at the studio throughout the evening, conducting interviews; the last car was to be waiting as *RHS* ended, so the cast members from that show could pile in and be driven to Pinkafeld at top speed. Conny was to be a passenger in that car, armed with creams and water to remove Aidan's fantastic Riff Raff makeup as the car sped along so that he could sing 'Meadowlark' straight.

However, several of those who should have travelled in the early car failed to show up on time, and I was sent in that first one, to leave extra places for the later transport. So I arrived at the studio in the early evening, glittering dress and gold evening sandals again, knowing little German and no one there; my fellow-passenger singers retired to their nearby hotel rooms to change and rehearse. Champagne was flowing – or rather, a sparkling wine known as Sekt. Being asked in an Austrian accent if I would like some Sekt, I interpreted it phonetically and was, to say the least, surprised. However, through the four hours while I waited trustfully for my son to appear and claim me, wondering whereabouts in Austria I was, and gazing at the high-tech control desks, most screens showing Kim Duddy undulating, my glass was frequently refilled. It was during those hours that I decided to write this book. And yes, Aidan did arrive, and after greeting his mother, pulled a condom over his bald head and blew it up on the platform as finale to the *Musical? Oh My God* ... excerpts.

On the Saturday of that eventful week, two days later, there was a theatre festival in a marketplace, with platforms erected for open-air entertainment. Songs from musicals currently playing in Vienna were to be performed by the casts, including five from *The Rocky Horror Show*. Conny and I were in the crowd pressing round the platform. Alexander Goebel announced the first three songs in German, and they were duly performed by the cast we knew. Aidan was due to sing next: Alexander spoke for a while more, finally calling, 'Riff Raff!'—and on came a figure in Riff Raff's costume and wig who was not Aidan. I felt utter consternation – why was a substitute for Aidan necessary? – until Conny explained that there had been a Riff Raff look-alike competition, and Alexander had been announcing and presenting the winner. Aidan then came on and belted out 'The Time Warp': his first experience of open-air rock.

Conny and I, due to eat with him afterwards, had to wait some time while he autographed his way through the crowd.

Aidan was organizing an eight-hour 'Starathon' for charity, with performers each to do a fifteen-minute act, free. During my visit, he was persuading all those he knew

Aidan's party trick at the
X-ART studio launch,
1993

to do a turn: cast members from *Musical?—Oh My God ..., Freudiana*, the about-to-open *Kiss of the Spider Woman*: colleagues from the English Theatre in Vienna; children's dancing classes. The greatest problem was to find enough free pianists to accompany the acts. Aidan opened the show as Margaret; Michael Reardon from *Musical?—Oh My God ...* did a stunning Liza Minnelli; ladies from Blue Danube Radio performed Joyce Grenfell monologues and 'Nobody loves a fairy when she's forty'. The wine bar stayed crowded throughout, and Romanian orphanages benefited to the tune of 70,000 schillings.

The event was to be held on a Sunday, from 2 to 10 p.m., the day after my return flight to England was booked. I longed to perform in the Starathon myself—was not my own theatre comeback long overdue? I contemplated doing 'Rose's Turn' from *Gypsy*: Rose being the domineering mother of Louise (the young Gypsy Rose Lee), constantly shouting to her daughter at her auditions, 'Sing out, Louise!'. My flight home could not be changed, though, so Aidan was not put to the point of deciding whether he would allow his mother to sing in his show.

Back in England I went to see *Carousel* at the Shaftesbury Theatre. In the final scene, the father of the sad, silent Louise of that show returns from the dead to attend her graduation ceremony, and spectrally urges her to join in the choral singing of 'When You Walk Through a Storm'. My head still full of Rose, I could hardly forbear to leap from my seat and cry, 'Sing out, Louise!'

For the second day after *RHS*'s six-week run ended, Aidan was offered two prestigious and well-paid appearances – to do solo cabaret at one of Vienna's universities, and at a corporate event in Salzburg, three hours' drive away. He was determined to accept both engagements, but neither date could be altered; both were for appearances at specific, pre-arranged events. He had done several car presentations for Fiat (one in costume as a crash dummy, reproduced as a poster), and used his

83

contact there to obtain a fast car and driver for two days. He persuaded the organizers of the Salzburg occasion (a conference of McDonald managers – providers of the Frank'N'Burgers at the *Rocky Horror* after-show party) to allow him to perform to them in the morning, so that he could finish at midday.

The day after *RHS*'s last night and party he was driven to Salzburg. There, the next morning, he sang 'The Time Warp' to the McDonald managers. At midday, with Conny in attendance to help again with in-car costume changes, he was driven by Fiat at full tilt to arrive at the university with five minutes in hand before performing half an hour's solo cabaret for a student presentation, starting at three o'clock.

Aidan took on a variety of productions and projects: produced a series of 'artists unplugged' (no sound amplification); repeated his one-man show in various venues; Margaret was much seen about town. He posed for more commercials: for one, not certain if he had the right expression, wanting to check with the photographer, but unable to recall the German word for 'expression', he asked in German literally, 'Is this face all right?'. 'Why, do you have another one?' the photographer asked.

He was acquiring fans, even a fan club – 'Clappers'. One anonymous fan took to leaving gifts outside his flat in Vienna (up three high flights of stairs, no lift). He would open his front door to find surprise presents, such as boxes of tea; at Easter, an elaborate hanging decoration; on his birthday, thirty yellow roses, an iced cake representing his head as on his posters, a cushion screen-printed with his image.

Replying to the friendly enquiry, 'What's your younger son doing now?' became as complicated for me as answering the small-talk question I am most often asked and most dread, 'Tell me, I've never quite understood—what exactly does an indexer do?'

Aidan was much recognized in Vienna now, being greeted once in a restaurant by a Chinese waiter with, 'You are Liff-Laff in Locky Hollor Show!' The gratifying plethora of offers as well as requests that he now received meant that choices had to be made, work sometimes refused. He even turned down, twice, the chance to sing in *Jesus Christ Superstar* in Switzerland. Who would have thunk it, in those teenage fan-worshipful years?

Aidan was also planning the production of a CD-album of his singer-lodger, Aris Sas, then a teenager with angel face and powerful voice, doomed so far to playing pathetic urchins—Gavroche in *Les Misérables,* Little John in *West Side Story*, Jack in *Into the Woods*. He told me he yearned to sing 'The American Dream', the engineer's raunchy song from *Miss Saigon*. 'You don't look corrupt enough', I pointed out. '*Not yet*', he declared with relish.

Aidan was adding the role of impresario to those of actor, composer, and singer. He was one of the first users of a (very expensive, then) mobile phone. The time he spent with it clamped to his ear, at tables, in cars or buses or proceeding along pavements, exceeded that available to return calls at home. Laptop computer, now available, always at hand, he became a one-man peripatetic office.

I flew to Vienna again to see the repeat of his one-man show, *Who the Hell is Aidan Bell?*. His flat at this time contained, as well as himself, two cats, singing lodger and lodger's girl-friend; Conny, in Vienna to help with this production, and looking for theatre work to enable her to remain there; and Noel Stevens with fellow musicians.

Noel was now living in Cologne, another non-German-speaking English musician settling in a German-speaking country to work, often driving the 555 miles to Vienna to play for Aidan's shows. I would have to resort to staying in a hotel for this visit – no room in the flat – and made it only for three days, to catch both performances and return. I felt very much a jet-setter, though without the appropriate income. On arrival I found the town plastered with posters and postcards advertising the show, displaying Aidan's bald-head logo. (I congratulated myself, as often before, on having bestowed on him a short name whose letters could appear large on posters.) Friends from Hatfield on a Viennese holiday were astonished to see these posters enquiring who was Aidan Bell, and attended the show, surprising us in turn.

For the last two weeks of December 1993, Aidan starred in *Christmas Bells*, in the Residenz Theatre, directed by Conny, with five familiar fellow-performers, and a different guest artiste each night. After playing on the evening of 23rd December, Aidan flew to London on the afternoon of Christmas Eve, spent Christmas Day with us in Hatfield, and flew back to Vienna on the morning of 26th to appear in *Christmas Bells* again that night. Next day, 27th December, a fax came through: a cutting from a Viennese newspaper with a photograph of Aidan and his own translation of the text:

> Aidan Bell, unforgettable Riff Raff from the Viennese 'Rocky Horror Show' production, flew to his home in London for just 36 hours in order to embrace his mother before the end of the year. Before this, he was at the Virgin Megastore in Mariahilferstraße to sing for his fans his aptly-titled 'Christmas Bells'.

That was a high for a stage mother.

Aidan spent several weeks in early 1994 staying in Pinkafeld with Jerry Pacher, the Chief Engineer of X-ART Studios, producing his first solo CD, *Timewarp*. I received a long fax requesting me to obtain and urgently despatch to him the full orchestrated scores or, failing that, complete vocal scores of *Chess, Evita* and *Into The Woods*, which, he told me, might be available only for rent from specialist shops in London. This caused me much difficult searching and telephone calls, on another unfamiliar quest.

He sang eleven songs on the CD, opening with 'The Time Warp', and including three of his own composition, two from *Elite*. As well as composer and performer, Aidan was also Assistant Engineer and played additional keyboards and additional percussion. Noel Stevens – by then designated by Aidan, 'Saint Noel of Cologne' – was responsible for keyboards, arrangements and synth programming. Diana, beginning another career move to become a singer herself, also stayed in Pinkafeld for a week as production assistant, and sang as one of the background vocalists.

The *Timewarp* CD was launched on Aidan's thirtieth birthday, May Day 1994. The party and presentation took place at Vienna's City Club complex, a huge glass pyramid housing a water park with several swimming pools, one, heated, outside, connected by water tunnels and slides. We all flew out *en famille* for the occasion, Ian bringing a rain stick to enhance his dancing at the party. Diana spent the day exercising her theatre management skills in overseeing the blowing up and arrangement of 2000 red and black balloons and display of 800 posters around the club, and her nanny skills in discouraging children from removing the balloons as they left the swimming pool; in the evening she switched role and performed as backing singer on the platform in the main swimming pool to Aidan's performance before the 250 or so guests, press and TV cameras, of 'The Time Warp' and 'The Rum Tum Tugger' from the CD. The

The under water Time Warp, 1994

band was led (but of course) by Noel. After two more songs from the CD, the audience saw probably the world's only underwater version of 'The Time Warp', with Aidan in Riff Raff butler costume singing *in* the pool, and a chorus who started dancing on the platform and finished in the water – though a very different affair from Busby Berkeley's water ballets.

26 Dear Mrs Worthington . . .

Don't put your daughter on the stage, Mrs Worthington,
Don't put your daughter on the stage

Noël Coward's famous counsel to Mrs Worthington is gradually revealed to be due to the fact that 'the wretched girl', her unfortunate daughter, is 'a bit of an ugly duckling', broad-beamed, squinting, with dreary personality and voice 'not exactly flat'. One can see his point. But I dissociate myself from the lady: my own stage-strider being male, and definitely talented; and likewise from those other notorious stage mothers, the battling Rose from *Gypsy*, and Mrs Crummles in Dickens's *Nicholas Nickleby*, mother of the balletic Infant Phenomenon who 'had been kept up late every night, and put upon an unlimited allowance of gin-and-water from infancy, to prevent her growing tall'.

But, given a child actually endowed with theatre talent, what advice might one best offer *la vraie* Mrs Worthington?

To start with, *no one* can *put* their child onto the stage. Anyone sufficiently biddable to be *put* into any career would lack the essential strength of character needed to get anywhere in this most crowded, competitive profession, where so much depends on basic personal integrity. One can only watch, pray, grieve over or marvel at the doings of one's theatrical young.

As a mother who for a while had two children established in more conventional careers and one on the stage, perhaps I can offer counsel. At the time of the great party in Vienna, my eldest and youngest were alike happily living with their apparent lifelong partners, steadily paying their mortgages, enjoying regular earned income, within reasonable driving distance of the parental home. Aidan, by contrast, lived hand-to-mouth in a state of permanent financial crisis, frenetically active, never knowing what he would be doing where three months ahead, an expensive over-two-hours' flight away from his family, where none of us spoke the language. Conny would not be able to join him permanently until he had a settled abode where she too might find theatre work. We did not know what was to develop for him: maybe he would die unknown; maybe I was to be known only as 'the mother of Aidan Bell'.

There are rewards, though. 'You must be proud of him!' so many people have said to me. Well, of course. One sees one's child in the cradle, the bath, the playpen, playgroup, schoolroom, shops—later behind the wheel, at the desk, at social occasions. Viewing one's young aloft on stage, behind footlights, across a crowded auditorium, gives a whole new perspective and glow. The sense of vicarious personal

87

Aidan and his proud mother after *Who the Hell Is Aidan Bell?* 1993

achievement may be false – 'to think that the way I washed the dishes led to this magnificence!'—but is nevertheless wholly satisfactory. Seeing your offspring in so many alien guises makes you feel, like Jane Wyman's Nanny, 'Mother to dozens'—each one cherished.

Success and fulfillment cannot, of course, be guaranteed; but when it's good, it's great.

Let it be, Mrs W. If they're determined and talented, they gotta do what they gotta do; there's nothing you can do to curb it. You may find, though, that *you* gotta do some most unexpected and uncharacteristic things in consequence.

P. S. When one's child attains his 31st year, motherhood surely becomes less fraught, its responsibilities diminished. I felt myself thereafter no longer such a hostage to theatrical fortunes, able to concentrate more intently upon my own career. This chronological landmark for the son – almost a rite of passage for the mother – seems an appropriate place to close this narrative of clashing ways of life, so I will not go on to record how Aidan left Vienna after seven crowded years there and returned to England, and married Conny on a ship on the Danube; and how Diana in her turn became a singer and radio presenter working in Greece and Cyprus, and Ian took to body-painting and breeding Burmese cats ... However, much of what has befallen Aidan, and all the family since the great party can be followed on the website he subsequently set up:

www.aidanbell.com

Index

Note: Page numbers in *italics* indicate illustrations

accidents
  car 19, 65
  at home 20
  in theatre 33
advertisements 27, *27, 28*, 84
Aesop 21-2, 40, 45
agents 29, 59-61
Aikido 26
airports 49, 63-4
Aladdin 31
Amstetten, Austria 72, 74-5
Andersen, Hans 72
Ankara, Nikki 45
answerphones 20, 63, 66
  agents' 60
Apollo Victoria Theatre, London 24-6
auditions 22, 45, 56-7
  The Rocky Horror Show 60-2
Austrian Embassy 67

baby shoots 46
baldness 73-4, 80, *81*
Barber, Lewis 32
Barlow, Patrick 31, *31*
Baxter, Stanley 31, 77
Bell, Colin 8, 9, 13, 14, 20, 23, 28, 33, 37, 39, 51, 68, 74-5
Bell, Diana 5, 20, 22, 29, *32*, 35, 37, 39, 40, 45, 52-3, 58, 61, 62, 63-5, *64*, 66, 67, 68, 86, 88
  chaperone 37-8, 46-7
  in London 47-8, 63
Bell, Ian 8, 9, 20, 22, 26, 29, 37, 86, 88
'Elite' 35, *36*, 37, 40, 41
Berlin 52, 74
Bernadette 45
Billy 13, 15
Blood Brothers 47
Blue Danube radio 68, 71, 83
Blues Brothers 33

Bognor Regis, Sussex 6-8
Bond, Gary 15-16
Braben, David 35, 37
Branchline Theatre Company 19
Bristol Hippodrome 17
Bristol Old Vic 29-30
Brownlie, Morag 48
Budapest 62-3, 64-5

cabaret 55-6, 74, 83-4
Camelot 25
Card in a Window 41, 44, 45
Carousel 80, 83
cars 34, 56, 68
  accidents 19, 65
  insurance 28
  searched 52
casting 58-62
chaperones 37-8, 46-7
Chapman, Mark 17
Chess 41-2, 86
child actors 32, 37, 46-7
child models 10, *11*, 46
Chorus Line, A 10, 15
Christmas Bells 85
Christmas carol-singing 12-13
church choir 12-13
Cinderella 47-8
clubs, London 26
commercials 27, *27, 28*, 84
computer games 20
  see also 'Elite'
costumes 10-12, 31, 80
Hair 49-50
hire 37, 66
man as woman 54, 65
Coward, Noël 5, 87
Customs 52, 77
CVs 58-61

89

'Dances from *Piper*' 41
dancing schools 10, 12, *15*, 37, 46
  seaside resort 6-7
demonstrators, in store 23-4, *23*
Denver, John 25
Department of Social Services 27-8
Devil and Mr Stone, The 45
Dick Whittington 29, *29*
diction 15
directories 37, 53, 66
Donmar Warehouse 45, 57
Drama Schools 21
drug abuse recognition film 27
drug searches 52
Duddy, Kim 72, 77, 82
Duncan, Kirk 21, 56
Düsseldorf 52-3, 56, 62, 70

Ealing 26, 43
East Herts College of Further
  Education 18-19, 20-2, 35
'Elite' (computer game) 35, *36*, 37, 40
  music 41
Elite (musical) 40, 41, 57, 86
Elmer Sands Holiday Camp 7
Elsinore, Denmark 72
Equity 19, 20, 22, 26, 28, 33
Evita 15-16, 56
examinations 20-1, 22

Façade Suite (Walton) 10
Falcheham Players 6, 7
fans 84
faxes 51, 66
Felpham, Sussex 6-8
ferries 34, 52, 61
Fiat 83-4
freelance work 20, 27-8, 57, 66-7, 79
Freiburg, Germany 38-9
Freudiana 53, 58, 62, 65, 69, 70, 71
*Funny Thing Happened on the Way to
  the Forum, A* 31, *31*, 43

Godspell 18-19, 80
Goebel, Alexander 72, 76-7, 80, *81*, 82
Gypsy 83, 87

Hair 49-50, *50*,80
  Continental tour 49-55, 56-7, 71, 72
Hamelin 39
Hamlet 50
  Elsinore 72
Hampstead, New End Theatre 29
Hans Christian Andersen 72
Harris, Rosemary 6
Harrold, Ian 41, 43
hat, Russian 74
Hatfield, Hertfordshire 5, 9, 12-15, 24, 28
Heathrow Airport 63
Heim, Conny 17, 24, 55, 69, 71, 87, 88
  and *Piper* 38, 39, 70
  in Vienna 80-1, 82, 84, 85
Hertford Symphony Orchestra 14, 31, 41
High Anxiety 77
holiday camps 7, 23
hospital 20
  Budapest 64-5
Huckleberry Finn 31

Ideal Gnome Expedition, The 33-4, *34*
indexing 66-7
'Ingenue, The' 51
Innocent, Harold 30, 45
insurance 28, 62, 64-5

James and the Giant Peach 32-3, *32*
Jesus Christ Superstar 16-17, 58, 71, 84
*Joseph and the Amazing Technicolour
  Dreamcoat 31, 33,* 56, 71

kazoo 21
Keeling, Stephen 42, 43-5, 47-8, 49, 57
Kelly, Terence 73
Kempson, Rachel 30-1
Kiss of the Spider Woman 57, 83
Kostas, Rudolf 38

language difficulties 39, 52, 64-5, 71, 78
lighting effects 57-8

Little Angel Marionette Theatre 10
Little Night Music, A 43-4, 45
Little Women (Alcott) 73
Liverpool 33
logos
   Aidan's 73, *73*
   Pink Hippo's 37
   Piper's 19, 39
   Lyceum Players, Enfield 24

Macaulife, Kay 6, 7, *8*, 9, 24
Mackintosh, Cameron 44, 71
Maclaine, Shirley 26
Maddie 44, 45
Magic Roundabout, The 67
Manchester 18, 32, 43
Manchester Library Theatre 31, 42
McDonalds 43, 80, 84
midwives 9
Mikado, The 10
Milton Keynes 27, 28, 35
Minnelli, Liza 24, 25, 83
Miss Saigon 45, 69, 84
Modelling and Acting for Kids (Hally) 46-7
models, child 10, *11*, 46
'Modern Musical, The' (radio series) 68, 71
Mother Goose 30, *30*
mothers and motherhood 41, 42
   of child models 10, 46
   stage 30-1, 47, 77-8, 87-8
   working 66-7
Musical? — Oh My God ... 76-8, 82, 83
'My Conviction' 53, 54, 55

'Nessun dorma' 56, 72
New York Police 17
Nicholas Nickleby (Dickens) 87
nodule, throat 34

Oberreute, Germany 69-70
O'Brien, Richard 73, 80, *81*
Odense, Denmark 72
Oklahoma 8, 17
On Location 22, 38
Oxford 44

Pacher, Jerry 85
passports 52-3, 56
Pavarotti, Luciano 58
Phantom of the Opera, The 48, 49
   in Vienna 70, 72, 76, 77, 80
Phillips, Brian 19, 21, 40-1
photographs 10, 19, 22-3, 49, 84
pianos 13-14
Pickford, Dennis 45
Pink Hippo Productions 37, 42, 58, 66
   The Devil and Mr Stone 45
   Piper 37-8, *38*, 41, 46, 70
   The Rocky Horror Show 58-63, 64, *64*, 65, 72, 73
Pinkafeld, Austria 82, 85-6
Piper 19, 35, 39
   'Dances' suite 41
   demo cassette 35
   East Herts College productions 19, 35, 48
   in Freiburg 38-9
   in Vienna 70-1, 75
   in Welwyn Garden City 37-8, *38*, 41, 46, 71
poetry recitation 7
Pope, Alan 45
Princeton, New Jersey 10
puppet shows 10, 19-20, 23

radio, Viennese 68, 71, 83
recording studios
   in Austria 82, 84-5
   in England 35, 40, 41, 42
Rice, Tim 16, 71-2
Rocky Horror Show, The 74, *75*
   in Amstetten 72, 73, 74-5
   Pink Hippo production 58-63, 64, *64*, 65, 72, 73
   'The Time Warp' 80, 82, 84, 86
   in Vienna 80, *81*, 82, 83
Roger the Robot 24
Romeo and Juliet 20-1, 50
Roof Garden Theatre, Bognor Regis 6, 7-8

Sadler's Wells Theatre 34

Salzburg 83-4
Sas, Aris 77, 84
school entertainment visits 19-20
school plays 14, *16*
security measures 25, 48
Seida, Michael 79, *79*
Sheerness, Kent 52, 61, 62
Something to Declare (Barnes) 61
Sondheim, Stephen 43, 44-5
song titles 68
Spufford, Francis 35
St Albans, Hertfordshire 12, 13, 14
St Pancras station, London 27
Stage, The 22, 23, 45, 58, 62
stage door keepers 16, 25, 75
stage schools 14
'Starathon' 82-3
Stephen Sondheim Musical Workshop 44-5, 49
Stevenage, Hertfordshire 43
Stevens, Noel 51, 54-5, *55*, 56, 76, 77, 84-5, 86, 87
stewards, theatre 24
Straker, Peter 42
Sutherland, Iain 41

telephones 37, 60-1, 62, 65, 66
  mobile 75-6, 84
  see also answerphones
television 29, 35
  children's 32-3
  commercials 27, *27, 28*, 84
  Viennese 73, 81
Think Yourself In 29
Time of My Life, The 44
'Time Warp, The' 80, 82, 84, 86
Timewarp (CD) 5, 85-6, *85*
touring
  children 47
  Continental 49-53
  in England 32-4
Truffaut, François 61
Two Ronnies, The 29, *30*

understudies 52, 54

Vienna 56, 58, 67, 69, 71, 74, 76-85, 88
  airport 63-4
  Akzent Theater 70
  Applaus Theater 76, 78
  City Club 5, 86-7
  Konzerthaus 78
  marketplace 82
  Piper production 70-1, 75
  radio 68, 71, 83
  Raimund Theater 76, 80, 82
  Residenz Theater 78, 85
  Technische Museum 80
  television 73, 81
  Theater an der Wien 53, 62, 64-5, 76
  university 83, 84
visa 67

Watford Palace Theatre 47-8
website 88
wedding in Vienna 56, 72
Welwyn Garden City 8, 12, 35
  Campus West 12, 28-9, 37-8, 45
Who the Hell is Aidan Bell? 78-9, *79*, 84-5
Wide-Awake Club, The 32-3
Wilkinson, Colm 17, 35
Willmer, Daphne 7
Winter Sunlight 26
Wizard of Oz, The 10, 12
Woodlanders, The (Hardy) 73

X-ART Studios 78
  Pinkafeld 82, 85-6
X Theatre, Hatfield 13, *14*, 33

Young Vic Theatre 12

Zurich, Switzerland 53, 57